Older Women: Surviving and Thriving
A Manual for Group Leaders

Ruth Harriet Jacobs, Ph.D.
Professor, Department of Sociology, Clark University,
  Worcester, Massachusetts
Research Scholar, Wellesley College Center for
  Research on Women, Wellesley, Massachusetts

This manual was developed under sponsorship of
the Gerontology Institute of the University of
Massachusetts College of Public and Community
Service, Boston, Massachusetts.

Family Service America
11700 W. Lake Park Drive
Milwaukee, Wisconsin 53224

Library of Congress Cataloging-in-Publication Data

Jacobs, Ruth Harriet.
    Older women: surviving and thriving.

    Bibliography: p.
    1. Aged women--United States. 2. Self-help techniques
--Study and teaching. 3. Life skills--Study and teaching.
I. Title.
HQ1064.U5J32 1987   305.4   86-32900
ISBN 0-87304-221-2

Family Service America
11700 W. Lake Park Drive
Milwaukee, Wisconsin 53224

Printed in the United States of America

CONTENTS

ACKNOWLEDGMENTS

I am grateful to the National Institute of Mental Health, the National Science Foundation, and the United States Department of Education for grants and contracts that have allowed me to do research on older women and to provide services for them. This manual was developed when I was chosen in 1985 to be a member of the first cohort of gerontology seminar fellows to be funded by the Gerontology Institute of the University of Massachusetts College of Public and Community Service in Boston.

I should like to thank the Gerontology Institute and the members of its first fellowship seminar for their assistance and suggestions. Also, I want to thank the women in the Anna Wilder Phelps Seminar at the Wellesley College Center for Research on Women for suggestions. Cynthia Stuen of the Brookdale Institute on Aging made valuable suggestions. Harriet Dockstader, Program Services Division of the YWCA National Board, provided excellent guidance and resources. I thank Family Service America for its support of this project. My thanks also go to Patricia Hamilton of Worcester, Massachusetts, who typed my manuscript. The Virginia Center for the Creative Arts at Sweet Briar and the Alden Dow Creativity Center, Midland, Michigan, provided me with working and thinking space. I am grateful to Janice Timinski for her editing of my manuscript.

Cordially and in celebration of magnificent older womanhood,

                                        Ruth Harriet Jacobs, Ph.D.

Purposes of the Workshop

This manual provides workshop exercises, materials, and techniques that are intended to help older women to survive and thrive in today's society. It is based on my knowledge of older women gained through research, personal experience, and leading workshops. I am sixty-two years old, a sociologist, gerontologist, and advocate for older women who has learned much from older women.

The workshop exercises are designed to help older women realize that what may seem to be their personal problems are really a result of the forces of sexism, ageism, and racism in society, which combine to devalue older women and even to make older women devalue themselves and other older women. The purposes of the first several sessions are to release older women from ageism and self-denigration, to raise their self-esteem, and to increase their awareness of the competence and capacities of older women. These early exercises aim to get the women to know and rely on other women as a source of support, friendship, and advice. Because of the dramatic gender imbalance in later years, often women must make common cause with other women. This may be especially important for new widows and women who have divorced late in life.

Since minority women frequently suffer from racism and other forms of prejudice as well as from ageism, ways to address their special problems are suggested throughout the manual. An extensive list of organizations that serve older women from minority and certain ethnic groups is included in Session Three.

Later sessions focus on the fact that deprivations and shortages generally are a part of life for older women, but that they can use various survival mechanisms. These can be employed to maximize what is available to them in terms of income, relationships, sexuality, self-development, community resources, medical care, recreation, and education. The goal of these exercises is to help older women to face the adjustments and role changes that occur in later years and to create vital new roles. Most women will make these adaptations eventually on their own or with help from friends, but a workshop can give them a head start and save individuals from having to reinvent the wheel or from depression because of self-blame or frustration.

The manual is intended primarily to help women of about sixty years of age and older who are living in a variety of community settings, such as alone or with spouses, in congregate housing, in housing for the elderly, and with families. Parts of this manual could be used with residents of nursing homes. The book is not designed for use with women who need individual crisis therapy or who are so economically deprived that their first priority should be immediate survival.

This manual provides some resource lists, such as the list of organizations serving minority women in Session Three, but it is not a resource guide. Rather, it is a series of very specific and detailed directions for twelve workshop sessions. A brief outline at the beginning of each session lists the objectives, materials needed, procedures, handouts, and optional reading, where appropriate. The instructions and handouts contained within this manual provide ample guidance for presenting a Surviving and Thriving workshop. The handouts are copyrighted, but leaders have permission to copy them for workshop participants. Suggestions for further reading are contained in the bibliography at the end of the manual and in some of the session outlines for those who want to supplement their knowledge.

A list of local resources might be useful for women in your group. Libraries, government, and voluntary agencies can help. A list of the kinds of agencies you could contact locally for pamphlets and information follows this introduction.

This manual is not directed toward helping older women obtain jobs. It is necessary or desirable for many older women to be employed, and thirty-two suggestions for older women seeking paid employment are included in the appendix. However, the Second Look project funded by the United States Department of Education has already provided two manuals for those working with displaced homemakers who need jobs and job training. Those manuals are available from the Superintendent of Documents, U.S. Government Printing Office, Washington, D.C. 20402, at

$2.25 each. You can request the Resource Guide for Vocational Educators and Planners, GPO #065-000-00010-5, and/or Vocational Counseling for Displaced Homemakers, A Manual, GPO #065-000-00020-2. Other materials and a newsletter are available from the Displaced Homemakers Network, 1010 Vermont Avenue, N.W., Suite 817, Washington, D.C. 20005.

This manual is not designed to be the prime resource for retirement seminars, as such classes must provide concrete information about financial matters and numerous retirement books and manuals already exist. However, the workshop exercises could supplement a standard retirement seminar by providing the extra assistance older women need because of the special discrimination against them. But it is most likely that groups using this manual will be made up of women already out of the work force. Perhaps many of them will have worked primarily in their homes. Nonetheless, the economic and employment status of the women in your workshop may vary considerably.

Obviously, great variations exist among older women in terms of such factors as ethnicity, marital status, life-style, and geographic region, as well as financial status. For example, the problems of urban and rural women are very different and so are the available resources. The workshop facilitator will need to adapt the suggestions in this manual to the group of women involved, and also may wish to incorporate techniques and exercises of her own.

Workshop Format

The workshop format provides opportunities for women to learn from personal involvement and their peers rather than from experts. However, a group or leader may wish to invite some outside speakers to discuss particular topics. The format allows for but does not require this. Session Three contains instructions for choosing speakers.

Although the manual presents the goals and purposes of the workshop exercises, the leader should refrain from announcing these at the start of the exercises. Rather, the participants should have an opportunity to discover for themselves by experience so that their learning is an outgrowth of what happens. The leader is a facilitator, not a lecturer, though she can briefly add her interpretation of the experiences at the end of a session if she feels this is appropriate.

Suggestions for Leaders

The manual is designed to be utilized by nonprofessionals as well as professionals. It is for any person who wants to gather a group of older women to look collectively at strategies for maximizing their strengths and resources in a society that is often not very cordial to older women. The initiator may be a community leader, a concerned older woman, a religious or layperson active in a congregation, a teacher at a university or community school, a volunteer, a senior center director, a club woman, a counselor, or social worker. Three book reviews on leading self-help groups in the June 1985 issue of Social Casework provide helpful suggestions for social workers leading groups. However, the main equipment for leading a group of women should be your own good judgment and flexibility and that of the participants.

The one thing people using this manual will have in common is that they care about older women, respect their life experiences, and like them. It is important not to patronize or reject older women. All exercises in the manual assume that older women are competent though they may lack information, experienced though they may be anxious, and capable of great growth though they may need support in the change process.

Publicizing, Forming, and Organizing the Group

A ready-made group may be found in a women's club or senior citizens' center. Or you may want to utilize local newspapers, television or radio programs, bulletin boards, newsletters, and posters to recruit a group of women who would like to explore surviving and thriving. Since older women themselves are not immune to the ageism that characterizes American society, you would probably succeed in recruitment if you advertised the group as "Surviving and Thriving Skills for Women over Sixty" rather than as an older women's group. Most people think that "older" refers to people much older than themselves. In the workshop, the women will have to confront their own ageism but you don't want to scare women away from coming to the group by using recruitment language to which they might not respond.

Notices or posters advertising your group could be placed in libraries, churches, temples, shopping centers, laundromats, senior citizens' centers and housing complexes, or other housing where many seniors live. Letters and flyers about the group could be sent to social service agencies, religious leaders, clubs, libraries, hospital social service departments, elder advocacy groups, women's groups, and ethnic organizations. Think about where older women in your community might see the notices. For example, if many patronize a beauty parlor that gives senior discounts, it might be well to put a poster or some flyers there. Perhaps a local chapter of the Older Women's League or Gray Panthers might want to sponsor a workshop, or perhaps the local YWCA. A sponsor can help by providing a mailing list and some legitimation. Put a notice on the local cable television channel or perhaps even make a presentation on a cable program. You might use radio or regular television to promote your group. If many older women in your community listen to a radio talk show, call in. Contact the local newspaper to see if they will do a feature article or at least put the group's first meeting on its calendar.

Word of mouth is powerful, so enlist some active older women in your project and ask them to tell their friends about it. Give them some flyers to hand out. Have a community center put a notice or other publicity in its newsletter.

Your group may meet in a school, YWCA, community or senior center, church or temple, clubhouse, home, or other setting. You may meet for fewer or more than the number of sessions outlined in the manual. If fewer, you can utilize those sessions that seem most useful to you and the participants. If more, you can go on to develop experiences that are indicated by the group process, or have guest speakers. Plan on meeting once a week for about two hours at a time convenient for you and the participants. The manual also could be adapted for an intensive week or retreat.

Do not be alarmed if you find a wide range of ages among the participants in the group. This can be very helpful as the oldest women provide role models for the younger ones. On the other hand, an age-homogenous group can also be successful.

It is important, however, to limit the size of the group. Generally, fewer than six participants does not provide enough input, and more than twenty does not provide each woman with enough air time or sense of involvement and comfort. The best number is about a dozen. Emphasize at the first session that regular attendance is important for continuity.

By the second or third meeting, you should provide a list of names, addresses, and phone numbers of group members to all participants so they can make contact with one another. This is especially important if any are ill and must miss a meeting. A coffee hour before or after can help group interaction. Certainly the cost or kind of facilities may prevent this, but providing a beverage or snack adds an element of sociability to the meeting. Comfortable chairs and good lighting help. Chairs should be arranged in a circle that is small enough for easy hearing and good eye contact. The leader should be a member of the group, not a remote authority, although the leader can, of course, provide information and resources.

Transportation and Costs

Since many older women do not have cars or drive, an attempt should be made to organize car pools or make other transportation arrangements if distances are involved or no public transportation is available.

In some workshops, participants may be charged to cover the cost of materials and the leader's time. In others, the leader's services and materials may be donated. A local business, foundation, or community agency might supply funding for the workshop.

Group Dynamics

Once the workshop gets under way, no woman should ever be pushed to share more than she feels comfortable revealing. The reticence of an individual should always be respected. Many older women have not been involved in encounter groups, personal growth groups, or in therapy. What might seem quite natural to certain leaders in terms of "opening people up" might prove disturbing or threatening to an older woman inexperienced in such situations. People should be protected from revealing more than they want. Should they say things they later regret, the leader should be available to deal with anxiety. Groups generally develop a high level of trust and mutual respect. But it is important for the leader to make sure that all the women know they are welcome to talk but also can pass and have a right to privacy.

x

Participants should be addressed by names they choose. Especially at first, some older women like to be addressed with the title Miss or Mrs. and by last name rather than first. Give people name tags at the first meeting to write the name by which they would like to be called. Respect this and make sure others do. If the women want to be called by first names or nicknames, that is fine, too.

The leader may be called on to exercise great tact if certain of the participants talk at such length that others are denied the opportunity. Forty-five percent of women over the age of sixty-five live alone and many have limited opportunities to talk and share their experiences. For almost every issue being discussed, go around the circle to give every woman a chance to speak. Be sure to note that those who wish to pass may do so. Techniques are provided in almost all the exercises for equalizing speaking time. But it is very important not to hurt the feelings of any woman in doing so. If it is absolutely necessary to cut someone off, try to say something like, "What you say is always so important and interesting. We wish we had more time, but regretfully we have to move along because of the darn clock."

A support group is different from a therapy group. This manual is designed not for therapy but to provide mutual help and support. That in itself may, of course, be therapeutic. But unless you are a trained social worker, psychologist, psychiatrist, or counselor, you will want to avoid going deeply below the surface. If you discover someone who is in crisis, you should be prepared to refer that person to a competent professional. Most older women, however, will have the defenses of a lifetime to protect themselves from getting more involved than is comfortable. But be very clear in advertising the group to note that it is not a crisis-oriented therapy group.

However, it might be useful to mention in your recruitment for the group that the group can help people learn how to overcome loneliness. Because of deaths and other losses, a great many older women are lonely. As leader, you might want to consult a 131-page booklet, <u>Preventing the Harmful Consequences of Severe and Persistent Loneliness</u>, available free from the U.S. Department of Health and Human Services, Public Health Service, Alcohol, Drug Abuse and Mental Health Administration, Rockville, Maryland 20857. Request DHHS publication number (ADM) 84-1312.

Evaluation

Before the halfway point, in Session Four, there is an exercise to evaluate how the group is going so that changes may be made as necessary. However, if you sense things are not going well at any point, stop and ask the participants to tell you what they feel is going wrong and how it can be fixed. No leader is perfect. No group can meet the exact needs of everyone involved, so do not have any utopian fantasies that your group can. But if a number of people seem discontented with the process, it is certainly time to find out why and to seek remedies together. Sometimes it can be something quite simple that may be at fault, such as a particular exercise that must be changed.

If some participants are shy about saying what is on their minds, use index cards to have group members anonymously finish such statements as "I do not like" and "I like" about the group's activities. However, caution participants not to use any individual's name or to hurt anyone's feelings, but to speak or write of the group process and the content of what is going on.

Keep your good will, empathy, and humor despite criticism. Older women have many deprivations and little chance to vent anger. If some anger comes your way or is directed at the group, realize that the person may have deep needs and a hidden agenda. Later on the individual may feel differently. Be gracious. Above all, try to make the group fun. Shared laughter is wonderful. Try to combine in the group a sense of play as well as of purpose. The group can be recreation as well as re-creation.

Lastly, remember that this manual is not meant to be followed slavishly. Read it through before starting to plan your workshops. Do not hesitate to omit, change, or adapt any of the suggestions made in this manual. Please contact the author to suggest revisions, additions, or deletions based on your experience. She can be reached at the Sociology Department, Clark University, Worcester, Massachusetts 01610, or at her home, 75 High Ledge Avenue, Wellesley, Massachusetts 02181.

LOCAL RESOURCES

The following lists many kinds of groups and agencies
through which you might obtain materials for or referrals
to your workshop. See also the list of organizations
serving minority women after Session Three, as this
includes some agencies that serve elderly women generally,
and the list of organizations in Session Eleven.

Area agency on aging
Area colleges or universities
Associations of social workers, psychologists,
  counselors, etc.
Community center
Consumer's guides
Counseling services
Day care programs for older adults (for parents of
  your members)
Employment services through the United States
  Employment Service or state or private agencies
  for older adults
Family service association
Free medical services or low-cost ones
Gray Panthers (see the bibliography for address of
  national office)
Hospitals
Hot lunch and meals-on-wheels programs
Internal Revenue Service, for tax relief for elderly
  home owners and renters
League of Women Voters
Legal Aid
Local association of clergy
Local chapters of the American Association of Retired
  Persons
Local medical association
Local physicians and nurse practitioners
Low-cost drug or fuel services
National Organization for Women local chapter
Older Women's League (see the bibliography for address
  of national office)
Police departments (for information on protection
  against crime)
Public welfare office for information on food stamps,
  for which some of the women may be eligible
Red Cross

Religious organizations
Retirees' associations and centers
Senior citizens' centers
Senior citizens' clubs
Service clubs, especially women's clubs
Services to the blind
Social Security Office
Special services of the cancer, heart, diabetes, and
  other health groups
State associations of older Americans or senior
  citizens
State department on aging
Telephone hotlines for the lonely and depressed
Telephone reassurance programs
Town or city department on aging
Town or city recreation department
Transportation services for the elderly
Visiting Nurse Association
Women's organizations
Your state's senior citizen booklet
YWCA

SESSION 1

STARTING TO KNOW EACH OTHER

BRIEF OUTLINE

OBJECTIVES: To introduce the leader and each participant. To elicit the members' current attitudes toward their aging and to explore the ageism within society and within themselves.

MATERIALS: Index cards, pens or pencils. Name tags if the women do not know one other.

PROCEDURES:
1. Leader and members introduce themselves briefly and mention their expectations of the group.
2. Exercises on three index cards. Discussion of the results of exercises.
3. Assignment to bring in pictures.
4. Closing ritual.

HANDOUTS: None supplied in the manual for this session, but you may have local information to distribute.

READING: If you want to do some background reading for this session, <u>Mirror, Mirror: The Terror of Not Being Young</u> by Elissa Melamed explains negative responses to older women and by older women themselves. So does <u>Life After Youth: Female, Forty, What Next?</u> by Ruth Harriet Jacobs. See the bibliography on page 129 for full citations for these books as well as further reading suggestions.

SESSION 1:   STARTING TO KNOW EACH OTHER

1.   Introductions

Your group may be made up of women who are already
acquainted or who are strangers to one another. If all or
some are strangers, you should first go around the circle
and ask each woman to say her name aloud and tell briefly
what she hopes to get from the workshop or why she decided
to participate and what questions she has about the
workshop. You, as leader, can set the tone for this being
done quickly by being first to give your name and
expectations, keeping your comments brief. You should
also answer briefly any questions that are of a factual
nature, such as how often the group will meet and what it
costs. However, if any questions are raised that should
be addressed by the participants as a whole, simply write
these down and say that the group can discuss these issues
at length after people get to know each other better.

In the event that everyone in the group is already
acquainted, you can, of course, omit giving names on the
first go-around but should still ask each woman to say
what her expectations are of the workshop or why she
decided to participate and what questions she has.

2.   Three Exercises

Next, pass out an index card to each participant and ask
her to write on this card what comes to mind when you say
the following words: "older woman." Explain that the
cards will be collected and shuffled by the best card
player in the bunch and that everyone will read someone
else's card. Point out that each woman should write
honestly the first thing that comes to her mind. It could
be a word or two, a sentence, or a paragraph. Ask people
to write clearly or print, but not to sign their names.

After all the women have finished, collect these cards and
have them shuffled by one woman. Ask her to hold them for
a little while or hold them yourself. Then give out
another index card. Tell the women to write on this card
the answer to the question "Who are you?" but say that
they cannot write their names. They can write a word or
two, a sentence, or a paragraph or two on whatever comes

to mind. Tell them that they will not have to sign their
names to these cards or read them. Explain that these
cards will also be collected and mixed up, and then
everyone will read someone else's card. When all the
women have finished, collect these cards. Again, have
them shuffled and ask the woman who does so to hold them
or put them aside yourself.

Then pass out the first set of cards, the one on which the
women wrote what came to mind when they heard the words
"older woman." Make a joke that if anyone gets her own
card, she should pretend it is not and that at least she
will be able to read the writing. Go around the circle
and have these cards read by each participant. Make sure
everyone reads loud enough for all to hear. Hold the
discussion of what was written until all the cards have
been read aloud. Then have the group discuss what was
written.

Usually, the cards will be full of stereotypes and
negative images of older women, even though the women in
the room are themselves older. The women will generally
be able to see this and point it out. Some of the cards
may not be negative, of course. One way to make this
clear is to take a count after the reading. Ask all those
holding negative cards to raise their hands, then all
those holding positive cards, and then the neutral ones.
Point out that in beginning this exercise you said the
words "older woman." Older is simply a chronological
fact, not a negative term, but that the word was seen that
way. Ask why. Ask why they wrote what they did.

This should lead to a discussion of the ageism within
society and the ageism within themselves. The discussion
should generate comments on sources of ageism in the mass
media and elsewhere and the double standard of aging for
women as compared with men.

If all or most of the women in the group had positive
responses on their cards, you have an unusual group of
women who are not ageist despite an ageist society or who
are trying to please you by writing what they think you
want. Comment on this and tell them how the cards usually
turn out.

After a reasonable amount of discussion, suggest that it
is time to read the second card, the one on which they
answered the question "Who are you?" without writing their

names. Have the second set of cards passed out. Go around the circle again to have these read aloud.

Usually, the women will have written really interesting self-descriptions. Ask for comments. Generally the group will conclude that many interesting people are present. Someone will probably identify some common themes on the cards or you can ask what were the commonalities. Someone will probably point out the difference between card one, which was negative about older women on the basis of age alone, and card two, which showed the women as interesting multidimensional people. Should this awareness not emerge from the group, you, as leader, can point it out. But first see if it can come out of the group process.

If you have time, you can do a third index card exercise. This is based on an exercise created by psychologist Dr. Robert Kastenbaum.* Ask people to answer the following questions, disregarding their birth certificates for questions one through five. Assure them that this particular index card will never leave their hands and they will only have to share what they want. The questions are:

1. You have the body of a what-year-old?
2. You have the mind of a what-year-old?
3. How old do other people consider you to be?
4. In your heart of hearts, in your soul of souls, how old do you consider yourself to be?
5. What age would you like to be?
6. What is your age according to your birth certificate?

After the participants have done this, ask how many wrote the same age for questions one to six. Probably no one did. Then ask for raised hands on how many had a five-year span among the answers, ten-year, twenty-year, thirty, or more. Most people will have a considerable span. Then go over questions one to five individually. Ask for a show of hands on how many put older than their age according to their birth certificates, or younger than

---

*Robert Kastenbaum, Valerie Derbin, Paul Sabatini, and Steven Artt, "The Ages of Me: Toward Personal and Interpersonal Definitions of Functioning Aging," International Journal of Aging & Human Development, 3 (1972), 197-211.

the ages on their birth certificates, or their ages according to the birth certificates. You will undoubtedly find that almost all put younger for questions one to five. Ask the group why. People will then speak about how competent they are, how they are in good shape physically and mentally, and so forth. Participants will begin to see and point out (or you can) that they have bought into ageism to feel they must say they are younger to be in good shape physically or mentally. It should emerge that youth or age are used often as pejorative terms rather than just as facts.

During this exercise some laughs should ensue. Almost always, participants give an age younger than other people consider them to be (question three). Someone will probably point out (or you can) that we all tell each other we look younger as the supreme compliment because there is so much ageism in society.

Someone (or you) may point out that for women lying about their ages or feeling ashamed of them may be due to the double standard of aging whereby women are considered less desirable at older ages than men are. The value of accepting your age as honorable should emerge in the discussion. Also some anger at social values should emerge. The triple jeopardy of those who are women, old, and members of a minority group should be pointed out.

3. Assignment to Bring in Pictures

Ask the members of the group who have access to magazines to look for pictures or ads that refer to women's aging and that show men and women together. Ask them to bring these to the next meeting if possible. You will usually find that women bring in ads talking about such matters as having young skin and pictures that show older men with younger women, or older men as vital and older women as not. Encourage use of publications such as Essence, Ebony, Black Enterprise, and Buen Hogar, as well as mainstream magazines.

If you have not had time to do exercise three at Session One, save it for the start of your second session.

4. Closing Ritual

Close Session One by reminding people when Session Two will be held. Thank them for coming and say that you hope

they will all return, and that you would appreciate any
feedback on the first session or suggestions for further
ones.

If you feel it appropriate, ask the women to hold hands
for a minute before you leave as a celebration of their
being together and as a promise of sharing and
confidentiality in the sessions to come. Whenever
appropriate throughout the sessions, it might be nice to
have people hold hands for a moment or so. Many older
women are never touched or never have the opportunity to
touch and it is good for them to have a tactile experience
of human warmth. If you do not feel comfortable with this
or any other suggestion, you can, of course, omit it.

SESSION 2

DEEPENING KNOWLEDGE OF ONE ANOTHER AND DEVELOPING THEMES

BRIEF OUTLINE

OBJECTIVE: To learn about one another's situations and shared concerns of older women.

MATERIALS: A wind-up clock or large watch that can be passed around the circle. Name tags. Index cards (if you did not have time at the last session to do exercise three).

PROCEDURES:
1. Introduce briefly any new members.*
2. Share magazine pictures brought in.
3. Divide the time by the number of women and have them tell their stories. Leader starts in order to set the tone. Save fifteen minutes for wrap-up.
4. Brief discussion of what was learned from the stories.
5. Closing ritual.

HANDOUTS: None for this session.

READING: Getting Older, Getting Better: A Handbook for Women in the Second Half of Life by Jane Porcino has a good bibliography if you want to do more general reading.

---

*It is not advisable to add new members after the second session, but use your own judgment regarding this.

SESSION 2: DEEPENING KNOWLEDGE OF ONE ANOTHER AND DEVELOPING THEMES

1. Introduce New Members

If anyone was not at the first session, have her introduce herself, and welcome her to the group. It is unwise to add members after the second session, so announce that the group is now closed. If you did not do exercise three last time, use it to begin this session.

2. Magazine Pictures

If you asked for magazine pictures and ads to be brought in, allow a few minutes to pass them around for comments.

3. Life Stories

Divide the remaining time by the number of women in the group, saving fifteen minutes for discussion at the end. Explain that members need to hear one another's stories. Ask participants to tell one another what they want others to know about their current lives, and whatever they feel comfortable sharing. Some may choose to pass and not tell their stories, or wait until the end. Make a joke of the fact that we could each talk about ourselves for months or write a 1,000-page book about ourselves, but we need a condensed version, so each person has so many minutes, depending on the number of women and time available. Explain that each woman, as she talks, will hold the clock so she can see how her time is going and pace herself. As each woman finishes, she is to pass the clock to the next person. Participants are <u>not</u> to ask questions, comment on what they've heard, or give advice, but simply to listen with patience and empathy to whatever each woman wants to share as someone who is experiencing the later years of life.

The leader should start the sharing. If the leader is herself an older woman, that will be helpful. But even if she is a young woman, she should tell her story first. Perhaps if she is a young woman, she has observed ageism and can mention how.

In the event that any woman runs over her time, the leader should point this out very gently and ask her to try to wrap it up soon. Point out that there will be more sessions and plenty of time for sharing personal experiences.

4. Discussion of Life Experiences

Several women may take an extra minute or two and there may be only a few minutes left for discussion. The discussion should be focused on what was learned from this group of stories. Do not focus on individual stories but rather on the shared themes. In other words, what are the common experiences of older women today? You might list these on a sheet of paper and save it for later use with the group.

If you have such a large group that all the stories cannot be told in one session, you may have to finish this activity at the start of Session Three and save the discussion for then. Some women may be overcome by tears as they tell about sadness such as widowhood. Provide acceptance, wait patiently, and don't panic. It is not bad to share sorrow. Hugs or holding hands can sometimes help.

5. Closing Ritual

At the end, remember to ask if anyone who passed now wants to talk, but do not pressure anyone. Also you may want to ask the group to hold hands in the circle, or ask each woman to shake the hands of the women on either side of her or to give them a hug. Of course, use your own judgment in regard to this.

Thank the members for coming. Remind them when the next session will be and that you look forward to being with them again. Be sure to get everyone's complete address and telephone number.

SESSION 3

PROBLEM IDENTIFICATION

BRIEF OUTLINE

OBJECTIVES: To have the women identify and prioritize their problems.
To raise the issue of special concerns of older women who are members of minority groups.
To have the women deepen their relationships and set up helping patterns in the group.

MATERIALS: A blackboard, flip chart, or some large sheets of paper that you can tape to the walls to write on. Pencils or pens and paper for everyone.

PROCEDURES: 1. Have participants list what older women need.
2. Have them prioritize these needs.
3. Decide whether or not to invite outside speakers.
4. Address the concerns of minority women. Distribute resource list.
5. Distribute other handouts.
6. Do vignettes and discuss them if time.
7. Ask group to do a homework assignment on giving advice and bringing in items to share.
8. Ask for volunteers to contact absent members.*
9. Close with a friendship circle.

HANDOUTS: List of names, addresses, and phone numbers of participants
Aging-Can-Be-Spelled Acrostic
Older-Women-Power Acrostic
Resources for Older Minority Women

---

*Continue contacting absentees throughout the workshop.

READING: <u>Library Services for Women in the Middle</u> by
             Peggy Glover has an excellent bibliography
             for general reading, as does the book by
             Jane Porcino mentioned at the beginning of
             Session Two.

SESSION 3: PROBLEM IDENTIFICATION

1. What Do Older Women Need?

Start this session by asking what do older women need.
Give the group a few minutes to think about this and maybe
jot down some notes. Then the leader should write on the
board or on big sheets of paper whatever people list. Go
around the circle. If anyone repeats what has been said,
add a number by the item so the group can see how many
women mentioned it. The list will vary depending on the
participants. But in most groups certain essentials will
be covered. They may include adequate income, good
housing, friends, recreation, transportation, good medical
care, information, sexual expression, being needed, and
good nutrition. List everything everyone says. Then have
the group look at the list, discuss it, and see if
anything is missing. Add it.

2. Prioritize Needs

Then ask the group to go back over the list and take a
vote as to how many are getting what they need in regard
to the various items. Vote on each item. But before you
vote, tell the group they can choose not to vote on any
item. Put checks beside the things most people feel they
have and X's beside the things most don't think they
have. If you have an unusually shy group, use paper
ballots for the checks and X's. Make a list of the X's to
talk about in detail at future meetings. (Future sessions
cover topics that account for many of the most usual
items.)

3. Outside Speakers

Ask the group if they want resource people to come and
talk about any of the most important items on the list of
needs or whether they want to talk about these issues
among themselves. If they want resource people, try to
find experts in your community to address the group, but
keep these outside speakers to a reasonable number so that
enough time remains for the group process. Group members
may volunteer to contact speakers.

If you decide on speakers, be very careful to find speakers who are both good and good for your group. In selecting a speaker, consider the following: (1) Is the potential speaker someone who would try to sell a service to the participants or be self-serving in some other way? (2) Is the speaker someone who respects and likes older women or will that person belittle and patronize them and injure the sense of self-esteem you are trying to nurture in the group? (3) Will the speaker fit in with the workshop structure you are trying to build or will the speaker simply provide entertainment and take up time? (4) Has anyone you know and trust heard that speaker or vouched for that person's integrity and knowledge? (5) Is the speaker connected with a reputable organization? (6) Will the speaker take the time to review with you what has been done so far in the group to avoid repetition? (7) Will the speaker go over with you ahead of time what she or he plans to say or do, so that you can see if this will fit the needs of the group?

4. Concerns of Minority Women

If you have minority women in the group, it is very important that they be encouraged to list the problems and tensions they experience. The poorest people in the United States are older minority women. Frequently they have other problems, such as difficulties in dealing with social and governmental agencies, lack of familiarity with the English language, or facing prejudice and social isolation. You may want to contact agencies that can supply materials or resource people to help with problems that minority women identify. One handout for this session is a list of organizations that may be helpful. Distribute this handout to the group members.

Even if your group is entirely composed of white women, do not overlook discussing the situation of women who belong to minority groups. Some of the women in your group may be in a position to provide friendship and help to minority women, and they should at least understand the special problems faced by minority women. This issue should be discussed again in Session Eleven, which deals with advocacy and community involvement.

You will probably discover that minority women in your group have even a greater difficulty in obtaining adequate housing than do other older women. You might want to supply these women with information about advocacy groups

in your community. National offices listed in the
resource list can refer you to local groups.

5. Handouts

After the group has done its own problem identification,
format planning, and speaker exploration, you can share
the Aging-Can-Be-Spelled acrostic, one of the handouts at
the end of this session. Draw attention to the list of
people's needs in retirement on the lower part of the
page. Participants may have overlooked something that
appears on it, and you might then want to consider adding
it to the list of priorities generated earlier. All items
on the retirement list will be covered in one way or
another, though, in the rest of the sessions outlined in
this manual. Also distribute the Older-Women-Power
acrostic. After the women have seen these, ask them if
they have any comments or questions about the handouts.

6. Vignettes for Discussion

If you have any time left in this session, you could
present some vignettes for group discussion. Here are
three ideas:

1. Lois, who is sixty-five, believes she has been
    denied an apartment in a desirable housing complex
    because of her race. What should she do?

2. Estelle has recently been widowed and stays in the
    house all the time because she is not used to
    going out alone. What should she do?

3. Lillian doesn't like people her age. But younger
    people don't seem to want to spend a lot of time
    with Lillian. What is the solution for Lillian?

In discussing these vignettes, or others suited to your
group, you may not come up with definitive answers at this
session but you will start participants thinking and
sharing their ideas on topics to be discussed again in
subsequent sessions.

7. Rules and Advice

Ask the group to bring to the next session some rules or
advice that they might give to older women. Ask them to
write these on a piece of paper and bring them next time

14

in order to share their wisdom that can help others get along. Tell them if they can't think of anything, that is fine. Request that they also bring to the group any books, articles, or pamphlets they think might be useful to others. They can write their names on these and leave them on a table at the beginning of the meeting. During the refreshment time (if you have refreshments) or before or after the meeting, group members can look at these things and perhaps borrow them or find out where to get them.

8.   Contact Absent Members

Make a note before you close of any women who are absent and ask for volunteers to call them to see if they are all right. Mention that the volunteers should not pressure them to come if they have decided to drop out of the group, but that the volunteers should say that people miss them. Have the volunteers tell individuals who were sick or had other commitments what went on in the session they missed, so they will not feel lost at the next session. Remind the volunteers to tell those who missed the session that members of the group are writing down advice to bring in and to please do so if they want to; also note that there will be a sharing table for books and pamphlets.

By this session, you will have provided all participants with a list of their names, addresses, and telephone numbers, so networking should be easy. Make it a habit at the end of every session to get volunteers to call the absentees, bring them up to date on the group's activities, and make sure they are all right. If anyone in the group should become ill, you will probably want to send a card from the group, so tuck a couple in your pocketbook to have ready for signatures.

9.   Closing Ritual

Close the session with a friendship circle of holding hands or some other gesture with which you and the group feel comfortable.

HANDOUT FOR SESSION 3

AGING CAN BE SPELLED

Anxiety **G**uilt **I**ncome loss **N**egation **G**roaning

O R

Activity **G**rowth **I**ncome adequacy **N**urturing **G**ratitude

Aging can be <u>leveler and loss</u> or <u>dignity and direction</u>.

The difference can come from a suitcase that gives
a handle for re-engagement in retirement.

Residence options--to move, where to move, or not to move
at all

Employment elsewhere--part-time work, volunteering,
consulting

Transportation and travel and trying new hobbies

Income maintenance and insurance information

Recreation opportunities and recognition

Educational opportunities before, during, and after
retirement. E is also for exercise postretirement

Memberships and community involvement--being needed

Estate planning and legal resources

Nutrition, health, and medical resource information
provision

Tax information and total planning

The suitcase is
heavy, so travel
s l o w l y .

Successful adaptation to new status
and roles

16

HANDOUT FOR SESSION 3

OLDER WOMEN POWER

Open yourself to different experiences.

Live each day fully. Don't postpone, procrastinate,
    please everyone.
Don't hold back appropriate anger. (It will depress you.)

Eat wisely and exercise regularly and get outdoors when
    you can.
Reach out to new friends and late education and re-education.

Weep if you must but then gather your strength and go on.

Organize yourself and your environment.

Mention all symptoms to your doctor and be insistent if
    that is necessary.
Eliminate nonessentials. Simplify. Fix priorities.

Never lie about your age to yourself or others. Be proud
    of your years.

Put yourself first. You deserve it. If not now, when?

Organize with others. Don't agonize alone.

When you can, laugh. Enjoy your age cohorts and younger
    people.
Express your sexuality and sensuality creatively.

Resist inertia, passivity, and stereotypes. Rebel,
    create new roles.

RESOURCES FOR OLDER MINORITY WOMEN

The following is a partial list of organizations that serve older minority women, as well as those that serve multiple populations, including older women who are members of minority and certain ethnic groups. Additional listings can be found in Minority Organizations, a National Directory, Garrett Park Press, 1982, and Black Women's Source Book, edited by Michelene Ridley Mailson, Center for Research on Women, Wellesley College, 1982.

Alpha Kappa Alpha Sorority (a black women's social action sorority with 75,000 members in 700 chapters in 46 states). National office, 5211 South Greenwood Avenue, Chicago, Illinois 60615. Telephone 312-684-1282.

Asociacion Nacional Pro-Personas Mayores (ANPPM), 2727 West Sixth Street, Suite 270, Los Angeles, California 90057. Telephone 213-487-1922 or 202-393-2206.

Association of Puerto Rican Executive Directors, 853 Broadway, 20th Floor, New York, New York 10003.

Black Woman's Forum, P.O. Box 01702, Los Angeles, California 90001. Telephone 213-292-3009.

Bronx Chapter, National Caucus and Center on Black Aged, Inc., 384 East 149th Street, #601, New York, New York 10455.

Chicanos Por La Causa, 1112 East Buckeye Road, Phoenix, Arizona 85034. Telephone 602-257-0070.

Chinese American Civic Council, 2249 South Wentworth, 2nd Floor, Chicago, Illinois 60616.

Chinese Consolidated Benevolent Association, 62 Mott Street, New York, New York 10013.

Chinese Women's Benevolent Association, 22 Pell Street, No. 3, New York, New York 10013.

Comision Feminil Mexicana Nacional, Inc., 379 South Loma Drive, Los Angeles, California 90017.

Delta Sigma Theta Sorority, Inc. (125,000 members in 727 chapters), 170 New Hampshire Avenue, N.W., Washington, D.C. 20009.

Hispanic Senior Action Council, 105 East 22nd Street, New York, New York 10010.

Institute for the Puerto Rican/Hispanic Elderly, 105 West 22nd Street, New York, New York 10010. Telephone 212-677-4181.

Japanese American Citizens League, 1765 Sutter Street, San Francisco, California 94115.

Lamda Kappa Mu Sorority, Inc. (600 members in 30 chapters), 35 Colgate Road, Needham, Massachusetts 02192.

Las Hermanas, 64 West Ochoa, Tucson, Arizona 85701. Telephone 602-792-3419.

Mexican-American Opportunity Foundation, 670 Monterey Pass Road, Monterey, California 91754. Telephone 818-289-2000.

Mexican-American Women's National Association (MANA), 1201 16th Street, N.W., #420, Washington, D.C. 20036.

Minority Health Fairs, National Health Screening Council, 3022 Q Street, N.W., Washington, D.C. 20007.

National Alliance of Spanish Speaking People for Equality, 1630 R Street, N.W., Suite 126, Washington, D.C. 20009. Telephone 202-234-8198.

National Association for the Advancement of Colored People, 186 Remsen Street, Brooklyn, New York 11201. Telephone 212-858-0800.

National Association of Colored Women's Clubs, Inc., 5608 16th Street, N.W., Washington, D.C. 20011.

National Association of Cuban Women USA, Inc. (NACAW), 2119 South Webster Street, Fort Wayne, Indiana 46804. Telephone 219-745-5421.

National Association of Spanish Speaking Elderly, 1730 West Olympic Boulevard, #401, Los Angeles, California 90015.

National Board of the YWCA, 726 Broadway, New York, New York 10003. Telephone 212-614-2700. Also local YWCA branches.

National Caucus and Center on Black Aged, Inc., 1424 K Street, N.W, #500, Washington, D.C. 20005.

National Coalition Against Discrimination in Housing, Inc., 1425 H Street, N.W., Washington, D.C. 20005.

National Conference of Puerto Rican Women, 1010 Vermont Avenue, N.W., #812, Washington, D.C. 20005, or P.O. Box 471, Ben Franklin Station, Washington, D.C. 20044.

National Council of Jewish Women, 15 East 26th Street, New York, New York 10010.

National Council of Negro Women, 1819 H Street, N.W., Suite 900, Washington, D.C. 20006. Telephone 202-293-3902.

National Pacific-Asian Research Center on Aging, 1334 G Street, N.W., Washington, D.C. 20005.

National Urban League, 500 East 62nd Street, New York, New York 10021. Telephone 212-310-9000.

North American Indian Women's Association, 1420 Mt. Paran Road, N.W., Atlanta, Georgia 30327.

Sigma Gamma Rho Sorority (350 chapters), 840 East 87th Street, Chicago, Illinois 60619.

Southern Christian Leadership Conference, 334 Auburn Avenue, N.W., Atlanta, Georgia 20312.

Southern Poverty Law Center, 1001 South Hull Street, Montgomery, Alabama 36101. Telephone 205-264-0286.

United Native Americans (UNA), 7787 Earl Court, El Cerrito, California 94530.

Women of All Red Nations (Indian), P.O. Box 84905, Sioux Falls, South Dakota 57118.

Note: In addition, the national associations of many religious denominations are concerned about older minority women. The National Council of Jewish Women, Protestant denominations, and Catholic dioceses may be contacted for assistance. It is not possible to include all such organizations on this list, but it should provide a place to start. Check with your local library and municipal elder services department for associations and agencies interested in the minority aged in your own community. Libraries also have books that list all American organizations with addresses.

National organizations that serve older persons:

American Association of Retired Persons, 1909 K Street, N.W., Washington, D.C. 20049.

Center for Understanding Aging, Inc., Framingham State College, Framingham, Massachusetts 01701.

Gray Panthers, 3700 Chestnut Street, Philadelphia, Pennsylvania 19104.

National Action Forum for Midlife and Older Women, The School of Allied Health Professions, State University of New York, Stony Brook, New York 11794.

National Council of Senior Citizens, 925 15th Street, N.W., Washington, D.C. 20005.

National Council on the Aging, Inc., 600 Maryland Avenue, S.W., West Wing 100, Washington, D.C. 20024.

Older Women's League, 1325 G Street, N.W., Washington, D.C. 20005.

SESSION 4

SHARING WISDOM

BRIEF OUTLINE

OBJECTIVES: To show the women how much they already know.
To help each other with general advice.
To provide an anonymous questionnaire for presenting problems.
To evaluate the group process thus far.
To set the groundwork for coming sessions.

MATERIALS: Pencils or pens and paper.

PROCEDURES:
1. Provide ten minutes for those who forgot to do homework.
   Have participants read or tell their rules or advice. Have someone put these rules or advice down in writing.
2. Pass out the first handout, Rules Regarding Being a Person for All Seasons. Have these read one at a time and discuss them.
3. Announce speakers' dates, if any.
4. Do a preliminary evaluation of the workshop.
5. Ask participants to think about meaningful activities that they can do as they age, as this topic will be covered in the next session.
6. Pass out the second handout so women can present their problems anonymously for help from the group.*
7. Closing ceremony.

HANDOUTS: Rules Regarding Being a Person for All Seasons
Anonymous Questionnaire

---

*In future sessions, allocate time for discussing the problems that will be presented on this form.

SESSION 4: SHARING WISDOM

1. Rules and Advice

At the last session, the group was asked to bring in rules or advice. Some women will have remembered to do this; others will have forgotten. Take about ten minutes at the start of the session for those who forgot the assignment to jot down advice or rules for living that they want to share. While some are writing, the others can chat informally. Then go around the circle and have people read their rules or advice. Discuss them. Ask the people whose rules are being discussed to write down the additional suggestions of others.

After this discussion, collect all the papers. Find a volunteer to type or write them up clearly and then copy them for the next session. Then, tell the group that they might like to compare their rules and advice with some from the manual on which their workshop is based.

2. Being a Person for All Seasons

Pass out the Rules Regarding Being a Person for All Seasons, the first handout for this session. Go around the group, having each person read one of the rules until all are read. Allow time for discussion or comments after each item.

3. Announce Speakers' Dates

If you have decided to invite resource people to speak to the group, announce the dates on which they will be coming and the topics to be covered. If you have decided not to have outside speakers, have the group consider the remaining number of meetings available and decide the order in which they wish to tackle the problems identified in Session Three. By participating in the advice and rule-giving exercise at the beginning of this session, the women in the group will probably have grown more confident about their ability to help themselves, and the group may now feel comfortable about proceeding without experts to work on mutual problems.

On the assumption that you do not have resource people, or at most will invite one or two outside speakers, the manual has workshop sessions dealing with major problems of concern to many older women. As part of your discussion about the way the group wants to spend its remaining sessions, list the topics of the remaining sessions. Ascertain which topics people want to keep or drop, and what they want to substitute from their own list of priorities. Encourage women in the group to lead some of the sessions, singly or in pairs. If they want to use the session format and instructions provided in the manual, copy the appropriate pages from the book for them. On the other hand, some may want to develop their own formats. Your group may have needs that cannot be met by any pre-established program.

4. Preliminary Evaluation

Since you have been meeting for a month, it is time to evaluate the progress of the group. This may be done anonymously, or you may ask the members of the group to sign their names. As Harriet Dockstader of the National Board of the YWCA has pointed out, "We believe adults should be encouraged to identify themselves in writing when they evaluate workshops because this act is partly an expression of responsibility." Ask the women to write on a sheet of paper their answers to the following questions. Emphasize that it is important to offer constructive criticism, rather than to target individuals or hurt anyone.

1. What is wrong with this group so far?
2. What is right with this group so far?
3. What can we do to improve the group and meet everyone's needs?

When the women have done this, collect the papers and mix them up. Pass them out and have everyone read someone else's. Let the group hear them all before you discuss them together. Decide collectively what changes to make.

As leader, don't be alarmed over criticism. Nobody is perfect and group process is never entirely smooth. You and the group can work together to try to solve the problems.

If you don't have time to do this evaluation at the end of Session Four, do it at the beginning of Session Five. Or

24

ask the women to write the evaluations at the end of
Session Four, so that those who write faster can leave
when they are finished. In that case, collect the
evaluations and read them at the start of Session Five.
Do not, however, ask people to do this evaluation at
home. They will forget.

5. Activities After Youth

If you are proceeding with the manual's workshop format,
announce that the next session will be devoted partly to
discussing meaningful activities that women can do as they
age. Ask the group to think about the activities they
have enjoyed in the past.

6. Questionnaire

Distribute copies of the anonymous questionnaire at the
end of this session. Tell the group that they can use
this form to get advice from one another about a problem
they may have, or a problem of a woman they know. Explain
that this will be done anonymously. Ask them to fill out
the questionnaire and bring it to the next session. Note
that some of these will be discussed at each session, and
no one will know whose problem is being discussed.

Not everyone will want to present a case. But have these
problem sheets available at each meeting after this.
Offer them to the group and cover a reasonable number of
the cases at each subsequent meeting. Of course, if the
women have little interest in this, omit the exercise.

7. Closing Ritual

Have your closing ceremony.

RULES REGARDING BEING A PERSON FOR ALL SEASONS

Everyone has seasons of despair as well as of happiness. These rules, or rather suggestions, offer some mechanisms to help you cope with the more difficult times.

1. Do unto <u>yourself</u> as you would do unto others. Too often, people, especially women, put themselves last. Recognize your own needs and try to meet them. Let others know your needs.

2. Forgive your <u>own</u> trespasses as you forgive those of others. Many women were socialized to blame themselves unmercifully and unnecessarily for small mistakes.

3. Realize you do not have to do everything and for everyone. Nobody is perfect--even you. You have feelings. Reach out to express them.

4. Set realistic goals and be prepared to change them. Society changes and so must we.

5. Realize that many of your problems, such as unemployment, underemployment, overwork, or loneliness, are not your fault but are the result of bad societal arrangements and structures. Social problems contribute to individual stress. Your difficulties are not necessarily due to personal failure or inadequacy. Band together with others for support and in an attempt to create better social and work arrangements.

6. Get exercise on a regular basis, such as swimming, walking, bending, stretching, or bicycling. Passivity breeds depression and tension. Humans need physical as well as mental activity.

7. Get adequate sleep on a regular basis and extra rest when you feel stressed.

8. Stay in touch with nature and the outdoors. Even in winter, dried grasses and trees are beautiful to observe. Allow for at least a short walk most days, even if you have to get up extra early or use part of your lunch time.

9. Take a ME day once in a while when you do things for yourself--personal grooming, errands, and tasks for YOU. In addition, take a BE day once in a while when you can just be and contemplate and enjoy.

10. Eat for health and not for recreation or expediency or economy. Your body does more than carry your head. Too much sugar makes your mood heavy as well as your physique. Good nutrition helps you resist both stress and junk food. Do not load up on coffee, other caffeine products, or excess alcohol.

11. Deal with your fears of aging and don't deny your aging. Go to your library for good books on this topic. There is life after retirement.

12. When necessary, ask for help from friends, relatives, or professionals. Don't always be a giver. Sometimes be a getter. You deserve this.

13. Build structure into your life. Too much time alone can be stressful. Even Thoreau left Walden. Get involved in activities. Go to meetings of organizations until you find one or more that you really like. Becoming active is one way to make friends, because shared activities provide a basis for friendship.

14. Don't worry about doing your work. Do it. Worrying takes more energy than the work itself. Procrastination corrodes you.

15. Go more than halfway to make friends. Other people are lonely and shy also, even if they do not seem so on the surface.

16. If your spouse or another important person in your life does things you don't like, don't brood. Talk it over. Mad turned inward means sad.

17. Grieve for your losses when they occur. Don't hold emotions inside. Then get on with your life. There often seems no justice, but we must survive. We also grow as a result of our crises. Work is good therapy because it occupies, integrates, and distracts us. Those whom we mourn would not want us to stop living. Those who have betrayed us should not make us betray ourselves by being mired in despair or anger.

18. Have fun whenever you can. Laugh. It is a good survival strategy.

19. Expect to be stressed and even depressed sometimes. Ride it out, knowing it will not last forever. Do not try to treat stress or depression with too much food, drugs, alcohol, or frenetic activity. Try some of the following:

    Explore what is bothering you if you are angry.
    Talk it out or write it out.
    Rest if exhaustion is the cause.
    Get out with people if isolation is the cause.
    Try vigorous exercise.
    Try meditation.
    Cry if you need to. Bang pillows.
    Think about changing your situation.
    Take a class.
    Think about changing your attitude.
    Get a good physical checkup to make sure there is no underlying medical problem.
    Get counseling from a qualified, objective person.
    Look at something beautiful.
    Do something for somebody worse off than you.
    Volunteer your time for a good cause.
    Call on friends, neighbors, or someone you trust.
    Realize periods of stress and depression may precede change, growth, and new directions.

20. To sum up: Retreat, regroup, rethink, react, revitalize, and run if you must, but also reach out, re-evaluate, and reason. Trust yourself. Stress is everywhere, but so is strength, your strength. Do not get too scared when you have low periods (we all have them) but remember you are recreating your life out of your struggles. COURAGE!

HANDOUT FOR SESSION 4

ANONYMOUS QUESTIONNAIRE

DIRECTIONS: On the back of this sheet, describe the problem of a woman you know who needs help. The front side asks for factual information about her. To protect her privacy, do not give the person's name or any identifying characteristics. It can be you. If you cannot answer some questions, write "don't know." The cases will be collected and shuffled so you will not be identified with what you write, but it will be discussed by the group so you can benefit.

1. The person's age is: _____

2. The person's occupation is: _____

3. The person's financial status is: _____

    _____

4. The person's educational background is: _____

    _____

5. The person is (circle correct answer): Married

    Widowed   Divorced   Separated   Never Married

6. What do you wish to say about the spouse (if there is a

    spouse): _____

    _____

7. What are the genders and ages of this person's

    children? _____

    _____

Copyright (c) 1987 Family Service America

8. What skills, hobbies, interests, religious involvement, friends, or other social supports does this person have?

_____

_____

_____

_____

_____

9. Presentation of the problem. Other characteristics of this person relevant to the problem may also be listed here.

_____

_____

_____

_____

_____

_____

_____

_____

_____

_____

_____

_____

SESSION 5

ADAPTING AND DEVELOPING ACTIVITIES AFTER YOUTH

BRIEF OUTLINE

OBJECTIVES: To see how activities can be modified or new
               ones found in later life.
               To handle some of the problems presented on
               anonymous questionnaires.
               To brainstorm about inexpensive goods,
               services, and recreation.

MATERIALS: Pens, pencils, and Activities-After-Youth
               Checkerboard.

PROCEDURES: 1. Collect questionnaires from last week.
               2. Briefly go around circle to see if
                   participants are having difficulty
                   filling time or are anxious about their
                   activities as they age further.
               3. Pass out Activities-After-Youth handout.
               4. Ask participants to share their
                   Activities-After-Youth sheets in groups
                   of four. Then come back in a large
                   circle for more discussion.
               5. Discuss some of the questionnaires.
               6. If you are not ready to deal with the
                   questionnaires, share information on
                   free facilities for recreation.
               7. Start a clothing (and other item)
                   take-and-leave table, if appropriate.
               8. Closing ritual.

HANDOUTS: Activities-After-Youth Checkerboard.
               Group members' rules and advice from Session
                 Four, if this was collected and copied.

SESSION 5:   ADAPTING AND DEVELOPING ACTIVITIES AFTER YOUTH

1. Questionnaires

Collect questionnaires about individual problems that
participants did at home and mix them up. Have someone
pull out a few to be discussed at the end of this session.

2. Present Activities

Next, go around the circle and ask people whether they
sometimes are bored or if they worry that as they get
older they will be bored, not be able to fill time well,
or to do the things they enjoy. As usual, let anyone pass
who does not want to comment. Some participants may say
that already they cannot do the things they used to do.
Give everyone a chance to respond and ask group members to
listen without offering comments or advice.

3. Activities-After-Youth Checkerboard

Then pass out the Activities-After-Youth checkerboard.
Allow fifteen minutes to fill out this form. Explain that
the upper section is for listing the activities that they
liked to do for their families, work, and
self-satisfaction in younger years. Mention that many
women have trouble thinking of activities they like to do
for themselves because they have been so busy doing things
for others. Nonetheless, ask them to try to think of some.

After they have done this, tell them to consider the
essence of these activities. For example, the essence of
downhill skiing might be exercise, adventure, being
outdoors, and being with others, as people rarely ski
alone. Ask them to think how, if they can no longer ski,
they might get exercise, adventure, outdoor time, and
companionship through some other activity. For example,
they could take bird walks sponsored by conservation
groups or city walks sponsored by historic societies.
Another example is that a woman might have enjoyed going
to concerts because she loves music, but can no longer
afford the tickets or get transportation at night.
Substitute activities might be to borrow records or tapes
from a library, to use the listening room in that library,
or invite a friend over to hear a concert on the radio or

television. Another alternative might be to ask the music teacher at a nearby public high school to let her sit in on orchestra rehearsals. Or she could query the local senior center or university about free tickets to concerts. She might offer to address envelopes and stuff flyers in them as a swap for concert tickets.

In regard to family, some women might have enjoyed nurturing others who are now dead or grown up. They might then decide that they can nurture needy children through Foster Grandparents or take on some other volunteer activity, such as caring for shut-ins.

Once the women get the idea of how to work with the checkerboard, give them about fifteen minutes to do so. At the end of this period, see if they need more time. Give them a few more minutes. If they are still not finished, tell them that they can do this exercise at home also, but to share now what they have been able to figure out.

4. Small Group Discussions

Ask participants to form groups of four to discuss what they have put on the checkerboards. Ask one person in each group to bring a summary back to the group as a whole. Suggest that each of the four persons in the group speak for a total of five minutes. At the end of twenty minutes, get back into the larger circle and have the reports from the "secretaries" for each group of four.

5. Discuss Anonymous Questionnaires

Use the remaining time in this session to talk about several of the problems outlined in the anonymous questionnaires. Tell the women that if they guess whose problem it is, not to let anyone else know. Also, emphasize that confidentiality is important outside of the group as well. Mention that whoever has presented the problem should realize that there are many points of view on a subject and that the group cannot offer definitive answers, only suggestions to consider.

In some cases, the group may decide a problem is so serious that outside experts should be consulted by that individual. Be sure to ask the group for specific, detailed suggestions on how to find the expert or helpful resources.

If a problem presented on a questionnaire pertains to material covered in future sessions, the leader (who will have read the whole manual) may, of course, utilize some information out of sequence. Or you could announce that later sessions will deal with this issue.

After Session Five, the leader should read all the questionnaires and sort them to use at particular sessions later. However, it would be good to do at least a few in Session Five, when they are first handed in. This will encourage those who have not yet completed a questionnaire to do so.

6. Recreation

If you decide not to do cases at this session because you want to screen and categorize them all first, you could expand the Activities-After-Youth exercise by brainstorming about inexpensive or free sources of recreation. Ask group members to share information about recreational facilities that older people can use. Encourage creative suggestions for off-beat activities. For example, many people get their exercise in the winter by walking indoors in a shopping mall. One group of women did this and used the mall as a park in which to picnic. One woman has discovered that a nearby town sponsors free showings of classic old movies in the public library. Another woman receives calendars in the mail from all the religious institutions in the community and finds many interesting, free events to attend. Tell the group about Elder Hostels, which provide low-cost room-and-board vacations at colleges and other places around the country. For a catalog, they may write them at 80 Boylston Street, Suite 400, Boston, Massachusetts 02116. Persons older than sixty years can also join American Youth Hostels for a small annual fee and stay at youth hostels for a few dollars a night. The address for American Youth Hostels is P.O. Box 37613, Washington, D.C. 20013.

7. "Share Table"

If the women in your group are not wealthy, swap information about thrift shops or other bargain spots in the area. Perhaps the women would like to share clothes that they cannot use by putting them on a "share table" along with books, magazines, or records that they no longer need. Any items which are not taken by members of

34

the group can be given to the Salvation Army or another charitable organization.

8. <u>Closing Ritual</u>

Have your closing ceremony.

By now the group should be interacting well and anyone who has not found the workshop useful will have drifted away. The groundwork has been laid for future sessions on more intense and personal issues. You may, of course, omit any of the sessions or vary the order in which you do them.

ACTIVITIES AFTER YOUTH

	FAMILY	WORK	SELF
Activities enjoyed in younger years			
How can the essence of these be adapted in later years?	FAMILY	WORK	SELF

SESSION 6

A SCENE FOR CATHARSIS

BRIEF OUTLINE

OBJECTIVES: To show how some women have handled aging.
To let women express emotion by identifying
with the characters.
To have four of the women express themselves
by reading parts.
To handle some of the problems on the
anonymous questionnaires.
To set the stage for the next week's session
on creative expression.

MATERIALS: Five copies of the excerpt from the play,
Button, Button, Who Has the Button?. (If it
is economically feasible, you might want to
provide copies for everyone in the group so
they can follow along as the play is read
aloud.) Name tags with the names and ages
of the characters in the play: Mary, 50;
Elizabeth, 60; Virginia, 70; and Dora, 82.
A large button.

PROCEDURES: 1. Explain the play.
2. Cast and perform it.
3. Discuss the play and what it suggests to
the audience.
Ask participants to bring in poems to
share at the next session.
4. Do some of the questionnaires.
5. Closing ritual.

READING: If you would like to read the entire play,
copies of Button, Button, Who Has the
Button? are available from Ruth H. Jacobs
for $12.00 per copy, which includes
postage. Her address is 75 High Ledge
Avenue, Wellesley, Massachusetts 02181.

SESSION 6: A SCENE FOR CATHARSIS

1. Introduce and Explain Play

Begin this session by announcing that the group members
will read and discuss part of a scene from a play written
by Ruth Harriet Jacobs, the author of this manual. The
play is called <u>Button, Button, Who Has the Button?</u>. It
tells the stories of twenty-one women of many different
ages and types. The scene that will be read aloud is
about several women who are much like members of the
workshop group.

In the scene, seven women, who range in age from twenty to
eighty years, share their experiences. Each character who
speaks holds a button which she passes on to the next
speaker when she is done. Explain that in the first part
of the scene, which the group will not read, younger women
tell their stories. The group will begin with the story
of Mary, who is fifty years of age.

2. Cast and Perform Play

Ask for volunteers to read the parts of Mary; Elizabeth,
sixty years of age; Virginia, who is seventy; and Dora,
eighty-two. Give the name tags and scripts to the
volunteers. (To help them, you could underline or
highlight the part on each script for the particular
character being read by each volunteer.) Note that a few
lines belong to other characters and that you will read
those lines, or you can cast the small parts for Lisa,
Ellen, and Jennifer.

Have the volunteers read the play aloud. When it is done,
take the button that the readers have passed from one to
another as they started their parts.

3. Discussion

Then, open the discussion by saying that it is time to
pass the button around the group to see what thoughts and
reactions the play brought up. Note that if any woman
does not feel like talking, she should simply pass the
button to the next person in the circle.

The play should spark a lively discussion. If the play arouses enough enthusiasm that some women in the group want to prepare a play or improvisations for future sessions, encourage them to do so. <u>Creative Arts with Older Adults</u>, a source book edited by Naida Weisberg and Rosilyn Wilder, provides some useful reading about drama. See the brief outline for Session Seven for bibliographic information about this book. In addition, ask whether members of the group have poems at home that they have read or written about older women. If so, suggest that they bring them to share next time.

4. <u>Anonymous Questionnaires</u>

Use any time that remains to discuss problems presented on several of the anonymous questionnaires.

5. <u>Closing Ritual</u>

As usual, have a closing ritual. Perhaps this time the group could say the "I Am Alive" poem, which concludes the scene from <u>Button, Button, Who Has the Button?</u>

SCENE FROM <u>BUTTON, BUTTON, WHO HAS THE BUTTON?</u>

(Excerpt from Scene Three of the play <u>Button, Button, Who Has the Button?</u> by Ruth Harriet Jacobs.)

<u>MARY</u>:   Who am I?

            I was a wife for thirty years. One day my husband decided he didn't want to be married anymore to an older woman, though he was, of course, four years older than I. I've always thought it had something to do with the fact that his company passed him over for a promotion. He was stuck in a dead-end job he hated while younger fellows were zooming past him. Anyway, he had affairs with women much younger than himself. Thank God our children were grown and out of the house. Finally, he made one woman half his age pregnant and he married her after our divorce. Now they have two babies and I suppose he feels important at home, if not at work.

            As for me, I remember going shopping shortly after he left. I kept walking around the market without putting anything in my cart. Suddenly, I realized I didn't even know what I liked to eat. For years, I had been buying what he liked and what the children liked and that is what I ate. I didn't even know my own tastes in food. How was I going to make a life for myself? Though I was pretty depressed that Sunday I went to a singles brunch I saw advertised in the newspaper. I got all dressed up. I guess I hoped to find a man.

Well, the woman who ran the club came up to me and said, "Please don't come back, you're too old for this group." I looked around. The men were my age or lots older. I was devastated. Of course, I had gray hair then. (SHE LAUGHS.) I have colored it since.

LISA: What did you do besides color your hair?

MARY: I cried a lot. At first it was utter despair.

           Leaving the suburb and wifehood
           for a cheaper city apartment,
           I moved my plants in first
           so something would greet me.

           The first morning I awoke
           at dawn to see the rats' ballet
           a strange and frenzied circle
           beneath my window and said,
           "there are worse things than rats."

      Strange things were happening to me.

           In what is one to believe?
           The city screams at you
           and you scream back,
           finding your voice
           someone else's shrill cry.

JENNIFER: I guess you were scared.

MARY: Yes and more than that.

           I envied those women
           whose husbands tucked them
           into cars and beds
           and paid their dinner checks.
           My so-called freedom
           felt like unconnectedness.
           I thought, some day
           I will stay in bed forever
           and no one will care
           or even know.

I hated married women and was foolish enough to
think they were all happy. Once, I even wrote an
imaginary letter to a suburbanite.

> You,
> with your small mouth
> and long tennis legs,
> living with antiques
> a husband and roses,
> don't know what it is
> to live alone on women's
> tiny wages that buy
> starches and roaches.
> Uncordially
> yours.

LISA: You had a right to be angry, I think.

MARY: Yes, and I wanted revenge.
           Before I saw my former husband again:

> I wanted to be loved
> or at least desired
> and possessed
> so that the creeping mildew
> of the soul and body
> would not be intensified
> by the sight and smell of him
> my lost and only lover
> of a long and wasted life
> destroyed by his rejection.

I covered up my pain with bravado. I thought:

> Not wanting to turn to salt,
> I won't look back.
> Salt is tears
> tears are acid rain
> and acid rain corrodes.

I told myself:

> There are other fish in the sea
> and I will fry them.
> There are other rocks on the shore
> and I will throw them.

>
> There are other men in the world
> and I will try them.

But it didn't work. There were a few nibbles but
I didn't land any fish.

> I didn't know how lonely I was
> until I met him.
> I said, "I am divorced."
> He said, "His loss is
> some other man's gain."
> I answered, too honestly,
> "there is no other man"
> and hoped there might be.
> He was silent then
> and forever, after.

ELLEN: Yes. Men are often afraid of getting involved.
          I know how you felt to be rejected.

MARY: Do you?

> Humiliating
> to wait
> at fifty
> for a call
> for a word
> for a kiss
> from a man
> hardly known,
> pushing aside
> proven women,
> fine friends,
> to chase
> his scent,
> knowing
> it is better
> to wait
> for a call
> never coming
> than not
> to wait
> or want
> at all.

LISA: Do you still feel that way?

MARY: No, at least not often. · I accept my singleness.
           It happened rather suddenly.

                 Once, passing a certain place
                 I joyously contemplated
                 being there
                 then realized
                 it was the sort of place
                 my husband and I
                 had often been
                 together.

                 For the very first time
                 I really knew
                 what all those legalities
                 had failed
                 to teach.

                 My marriage was as dead
                 as my youth
                 and all my mourning
                 and seeking
                 would not bring
                 them back.

           Since then I have gained strength. Joining this
           support group has helped. It was good I did
           because I had a setback when my boss fired me to
           hire a young, pretty secretary.

                 We will
                 work hard
                 for low wages
                 gratefully BUT
                 THEY much prefer
                 our daughters and
                 even granddaughters.

                 The unwanted cringe
                 our backs ache
                 our eyes dull
                 we even stop
                 thinking we
                 are worth
                 HIRING.

JENNIFER: I remember. You were pretty depressed then.
We had to help restore your self-confidence. We
nagged you to get some training for a better job.

MARY: It wasn't easy but I did take the courses. And
you all encouraged me through them and through
the awful job search. You, Jennifer, gave me a
good lead that led to a new job. It's lucky I
changed jobs because at my new place there are
other women alone. Doing things with them helps
me cope with the Noah's Ark Syndrome.

They are still coming
two by two off the ark.

Hostesses do not invite
unescorted single women
divorcees or even widows
expecting they will rape
husbands, steal homes or,
worst trauma of all, mean
an odd number at table.

What kind of orgies
need such pairings?

ELIZABETH: You make me feel terrible. It's true I
haven't often included my widowed women friends
when my husband and I invite our coupled friends
over. But I really thought the singles would be
uncomfortable. It isn't that I didn't want
them. As a matter of fact, sometimes when I do
ask one, she refuses to come because she would be
the only single. It's a two-way street.

Well, I'm sorry I interrupted you but I had to
say that.

I was wondering, did you finally get used to the
city?

MARY: It WAS hard that first winter. I didn't think I
would make it. But I did.

I rushed to the ocean
during the February thaw
to find dried sea grass
waving tall and golden
undefeated by the storms.
There by the shore
I danced with the grass
exulting at my strength
to bear aloneness,
shouting to the grass
"we have weathered
the winter
you and I
we are kin
we are kin
we are kin."

I felt proud of coping.

I have learned
to blow the horn
threaten landlords,
utility companies,
and meter maids,
use public parks,
thrift shops,
and free clinics,
insult insulters,
ignore accosters,
trust strangers,
when feasible
see rainbows
in the gutters
find in alleys
parking spaces
boxes for bookcases
wild flowers
even furniture.

Now I sleep through
neighbors' parties,
drown out trucks
with Beethoven,
fix doorknobs,
outwit pay toilets
swim at hotels
though not registered.

                    A new city kid
                    at fifty
                    learns fast.

               Well, I am sorry I took so long to tell my
               story. Virginia, here's the button.

(MARY PASSES THE BUTTON TO VIRGINIA.)

VIRGINIA: I'm glad things are better now, Mary. I used
           to think being divorced was easier than being
           widowed. When someone dies you blame yourself.
           You say, "what did I do wrong?" You feel guilty
           for living.

MARY: Women blame themselves for divorce too. They
           ask, "what did I do wrong to make him behave that
           way?" They even blame themselves when their
           children get divorced. Since we have so little
           power in the world, we overexaggerate our
           importance in the family which is the only place
           many of us are allowed to feel important.

VIRGINIA: I guess so. Anyway, I know a lot of women lose
           husbands through divorce or death. There are
           lots of widows around because men marry younger
           women and die younger. But it seemed at first as
           if I were the only one. I understand, Mary,
           about your letter to a suburbanite. We were best
           friends with our neighbors and after Ralph's
           death it seemed:

                    Wherever I went
                    they were always together
                    She was the echo
                    of his steps
                    and he drew in her closeness
                    like a fragrance.

                    Silent and close,
                    they dreamt by the fire,
                    spent as the embers,
                    simple with loving.
                    Watching their unison,
                    I yearned

for moments
that never again
would be
for me, for me, for me.

Oh, I did my share of crying too. I suppose it
is good I did. If I had to give advice to others
I'd say:

When a loved one is dying
go into the woods and cry.
Only pure beauty
like the sight of sun on water
or birdsongs in loved trees
that he will never share again
will bring those tears
for his darkness and yours.

The clumsy comfort of friends
and the strange running
or bargaining you will do,
will only make a tighter vise
about your throbbing head
and angry throat.

Go alone to beauty.
Mourn your aloneness and weep
for the loved one
and for yourself
and for the fragility of life
when the world shared
is so beautiful.

In the end we are all alone
but there is still beauty;
it is eternal
and so are memories
alive in us.

For me the memory of Ralph is very strong. I am
not a single at heart. I can't go to bars or
clubs alone as some women do seeking to end
singleness, at least for one night.

I know times have changed but I haven't.

I suppose I am still his.
Sometimes I have thought
the pressure of another body

                    would wipe away his imprint
                    but my desire flows backward
                    stubborn as the tide
                    to the wedding bed
                    so I wear his ring still,
                    cursing the throat lump
                    that certain music brings.

MARY: Weren't you ever angry at what happened to you?

VIRGINIA: Certainly.

                    Once I baked bread
                    and because I had
                    to eat it alone,
                    threw half
                    into the yard
                    for the dogs.

           I even went through a period of isolation and
           self-pity. I shut myself away, thinking:

                    Plants are more predictable
                    than people.
                    If you give plants
                    enough water
                    light and warmth
                    they will reward you.

                    People, on the other hand,
                    even given
                    considerable attention,
                    may forget you
                    or become hostile
                    or even die
                    Begonias are better.

           I was actually mad at my children and
           grandchildren for being occupied with their own
           lives. I hated the empty nest. I felt:

                    I had no home
                    there was no love in those walls
                    which enclosed my grief
                    no comfort in plants and colors
                    with which I tried to deceive.

                    There cannot be a home for one
                    where there had been many.
                    A woman alone becomes an orphan
                    crying in the night
                    with only cold walls to hear.

ELLEN: You seem all right now. It is hard to believe
          you were like that. How did you get to feeling
          better?

VIRGINIA: I'm not sure. Maybe time. Maybe my need and
           strength to survive.

                    One day I was ready
                    to give up
                    what seemed
                    an impossible life.

                    The next day
                    there was light
                    and air
                    and energy.
                    The dark had gone
                    as quickly as it came.

                    I could exult
                    again at music
                    and at the sight
                    of sun on snow.

                    The papers
                    I had thrown about
                    to signal my despair
                    could be put in neat
                    and manageable piles.

                    I could do
                    what needed
                    to be done
                    and what before
                    seemed a task
                    beyond endurance.

                    Even though I had lost him
                    I would not wear black

and put on Spring colors
being as I was meant to be.

Yesterday I mourned.
Today I have a life to celebrate
I have myself.

I realized it was not my fault Ralph was dead and
that he would want me to enjoy life. I began to
do things and take as many trips as I could
afford. If not now, when? I am luckier
financially than many widows.

At the slightest invitation
I bed down in strange cities.
From my lair in Bedford Square
I took London in a week.
Paris is in my harem now
and Aberdeen and Amsterdam
and Bath and Berkeley too.

New York and Washington are mine
I have dallied with Chicago,
San Francisco and Tucson,
Puerto de la Cruz and Marrakesh
I do not love you less
because I made Atlanta mine.

If I cannot have lovers
I shall have cities.
Sixty cannot be coy
as twenty with lovers
waiting in the wings.
I go boldly to conquer cities
Who is to judge of consummations
and compensations?

I also decided when home to get out daily for
exercise and seeing people. I joined the YWCA
and began to use the pool.

We are sweatless
and weightless
purity personified,
our rhythmic motion
comforting as we
unite with fluids

```
              of our individual
              and species birth.

              We are grateful
              for oceans
              lakes and pools
              where body merges
              intimately with
              perfect medium
              so even those
              unlucky or clumsy
              everywhere else
              glide and hide
              gracefully into
              crystal refuge.*
```

ELLEN: Swimming works off sexual energy too.

VIRGINIA: Yes, I know. If they knew how sensuous
           swimming was, they might ban it. I am in an
           exercise class at the YW too. Also, I made some
           terrific new women friends there including
           Elizabeth whom I brought tonight to this group.
           Elizabeth is a dedicated, almost full-time
           volunteer at the YW and other places. She got me
           into volunteering and that helped me too. The
           least I could do was get her into this group.
           And, now the least I can do is give Elizabeth her
           turn to talk. (SHE HANDS ELIZABETH THE BUTTON.)

ELIZABETH: Well, I've been listening to all your troubles
            and feel lucky that at seventy I still have my
            husband. He is special--a truly faithful and
            kind man. Not all men are like your ex, Mary.
            Our marriage has lasted fifty years. So far we
            have our health, are enjoying life and can help
            others. It feels good to be seventy.

                 Seventy is being outside
                 on a November day

---

*This poem was published in <u>Atalanta</u>, Papier Mache Press,
1984, page 35.

52
```
```

knowing the fragility
of sunshine.

Seventy is facing lost causes
and fighting on
having little to lose.

Seventy is loss
and dry tears unseen
but also passion
and private jokes
suddenly revealed by life.

Seventy is waking early
to seek treasures
which there is no room
to hold.

Seventy is sensing
which stranger
will give the ecstasy
of friendship
and who will betray.

At seventy
you grasp wisdom
in your hands
while they
are still strong.

Go into seventy
hoping and loving
you will be women
made beautiful
by having lived
well and long.*

VIRGINIA: You give me courage to get older.

ELIZABETH: Thanks. I've decided what is important in
         life. We tend to obsess sometimes about
         nothings. I'm beyond that now.

---

*This poem was published in New Directions for Women,
Volume 12 (September/October 1982), page 12.

Having climbed the mountain,
I came down the other side
carrying carefully mementos
collected with great effort
going up.

Halfway down I stopped
and suddenly hurled away
those no-longer treasures
amazed I had cherished
such burdens.

I have learned to live for each day and be
grateful for it. We women are lucky because we
love to nurture and can nurture through life,
though not always in the same way we did once. I
love being a senior volunteer and I love days
like the one I had at the beach last May.

I lust for the ocean.
In May when sunners huddle,
with shawls on the beach,
I swim the waves alone
warm with joy.

My sole ownership was challenged
when Amy, seven and a half,
introduced herself
and asked how to float.

"Don't be afraid
and you won't sink," I said.
She replied, "I'll play dead."
"Not dead," I told her,
"just relax--the water holds."

Neither of us cold
seventy swam with seven.
I taught her how to float
while her parents sunned
and Amy stroked my toes
in gratitude, teaching love.

Wherever you go, Amy
I shall go.
In the spring you are seventy,
you will recall

```
          how a May swimmer
          taught you courage.

          Though I shall be long gone
          I will live then in you
          my child and my sister.*

     Yes, life is good.  The only thing I worry about
     is that my health may fail or that Jim will get
     sick, or that I will become senile.

          Even my children grow old
          I see my years
          written on their once-soft faces
          now wise and worn.

     I hope at eighty I can still do the things I
     love.  Dora, what is it like to be eighty?  (SHE
     HANDS THE BUTTON TO DORA.)


DORA:    You are the same as you have always been, a
         little achy sometimes and slower and forgetful.
         Yet within you are all the things you ever were
         and more.

          Two years past eighty
          I forget a lot of things
          I don't want to remember
          like watching my words.
          I remember a lot of things
          I thought I had forgotten
          like Miss Brown
          who made kindergarten
          another home.

          Two years past eighty
          I own my old body
          with all its imperfections
          and like myself.

          Two years past eighty
          I spot a new bird
          learn a wildflower's name
```

---

*This poem was published in <u>More Golden Apples</u>, Papier
Mache Press, 1986, page 6.

```
see a great-grandchild smile
hear live, for the first time,
Bach's Sonata in C Major,
tell the President off,
drink a new wine,
and make new friends
of you.
```

There are lots of good things. However, the bad
thing is some people don't see YOU at all. They
see only age and reject and belittle you because
of that. It makes me furious when they talk to
me as if I were a child. Mad turned inward
becomes sad so I express my anger. I say to the
world:

```
I am in this old body
but not of it.
My mind runs barefoot
unwinded along the ocean
and my spirit climbs
mountains.

Who are you
to judge me unfit
and unlovable
when I so love
this world
and human touch?
```

You know some people never touch old people, as
if they are repulsive. When I was in the
hospital, I noticed that the interns and medical
students stood practically across the room from
me. And they couldn't wait to get out of the
room. It was different for young patients. Old
folks have the same needs as other people for
closeness. I let them know how I felt about it.
I'll make a prediction:

```
I will leave as I came
screaming pain.
I shall not accept with grace
the indignities of age
and the indignities to age
but exit--not too soon--
decrying my doom,
hating my fate,
```

```
                    protesting my loss,
                    pushing back the end,
                    with every angry breath.


ELIZABETH:  I like what you said.  I admire your guts.  I
            need to learn how to be eighty in a world
            insensitive to older people.  Can you be specific
            about how to handle folks when they treat us as
            stupid because we are old?


DORA:       I'll give you an example.

                    The electric company
                    overcharges me
                    but there is nowhere else
                    I can buy electricity.
                    I call to complain
                    they yes me
                    but still overcharge.

                    I will keep calling
                    and talking.
                    How much an hour
                    do they pay
                    their telephone clerks?


ELIZABETH:  Not bad.  It gives me some ideas.


VIRGINIA:   I know what Dora and Elizabeth mean about
            ageism.  I feel it already at sixty and get angry
            too.


MARY:       Certainly at fifty you experience it, as I told
            you.


ELLEN:      And at forty.


JENNIFER:   Even at thirty, the double standard of aging
            exists.  Men and employers bypass you for the
            twenty-year-olds.
```

LISA: At college, many senior men preferred the
         freshman girls.

DORA: Ageism is a common disease. You learn to live
         with it but you should try hard to do what you
         can about it. Don't wait until my age to fight
         ageism.

         Also, more young women have to prepare for aging
         by getting to know older women. I'm glad I have
         you all as friends. I lost my husband and many
         friends to death. A few of my friends older than
         I do not recognize me. But I have come to some
         reconciliation with my losses.

              No love is lost
              even though the lover
              turns away from us
              or life.

              Within us are the people
              we have loved,
              not as they were
              but as we wanted
              them to be.

              As our fresh grief
              softens to sorrow,
              we suddenly discover
              the lover's eyes
              in our mirror
              the lover's words
              on our lips,
              even the beloved's jokes
              have become ours.

              What reality has taken,
              we have taken
              for our own.
              Nothing is ever lost.
              Layers of our being
              contain all that has
              lived for us
              or that we imagined.

              We exude
              the strength

of our losses
and our gains glow
even in the dark.

All in all, friends, being eighty or even ninety
or one hundred is not bad considering the
alternative.

I'm alive
I'm well
I survive
I survive well.

Well, to survive as well as I do, ladies, I need
my rest. I think it is time to end this
meeting. If anyone has anything else to say, you
better do it fast. (SHE GETS UP AND GIVES THE
BUTTON TO LEADER.)

LEADER STANDS AND SAYS: MARY STANDS AND SAYS:

I'm alive   I'm alive
I'm well   I'm well
I survive   I survive
I survive well.   I survive well.

VIRGINIA STANDS AND SAYS: ELIZABETH STANDS AND SAYS:

I'm alive   I'm alive
I'm well   I'm well
I survive   I survive
I survive well.   I survive well.

THE WOMEN SAY IN UNISON:

We will rest together on our ambivalences.
We will share islands
as we struggle
toward an uncharted shore.

SESSION 7

TRANSFORMING AND SHARING OUR LIVES THROUGH CREATIVE EXPRESSION

BRIEF OUTLINE

OBJECTIVE: To encourage and teach participants how to express their feelings and share their experiences through poetry, journals, and other forms of creative art.

MATERIALS: Pencils or pens and paper. Something to write on, such as a table, clipboards, lightweight books, or pieces of cardboard.

Optional materials: copies of the list of poem ideas in session instructions (if a blackboard, large paper on the wall, or flipchart is not available). If possible, some poems written by older minority women or women from various ethnic groups. Also, crayons, felt-tipped colored pens, or colored pencils.

PROCEDURES:
1. Explore forms of oral and visual creative expression, if appropriate for your group.
2. Share poems brought in by participants.
3. Explain and give examples of list poems. Have the group write list poems and share these. Arrange for a volunteer to type and duplicate poems written at this session.
4. Explain journal writing. If time permits, have the group do and share journal entries.
5. Ask participants to jot down questions on sex and family life, an assignment to be done at home, for discussion next week.
6. Closing ritual.

HANDOUTS: "Love Brings Young, Old to Common Ground"
             from <u>December Rose</u>

READING: If you would like to do some background
             reading for this session, further research
             on the subject, or have more than one
             session on creative expression, the
             following books offer additional information
             and guidance:

             Alexander, Jo; Berrow, Debi; Domitrovich,
                 Lisa; Donnelly, Margaret; and McLean,
                 Cheryl. <u>Women and Aging</u>. Corvallis,
                 Or.: Calyx Books, 1986.

             Cobberly, Lenore M.; McCormick, Jeri; and
                 Updike, Karen. <u>Writers Have No Age</u>.
                 New York: Haworth Press, 1986.

             Kaminsky, Marc. <u>What's Inside of You It
                 Shines Out of You</u>. New York: Horizon
                 Press, 1974. Poet Kaminsky works with
                 senior adults at the Brookdale Center on
                 Aging of Hunter College, New York City.

             Kaminsky, Marc. <u>The Uses of Reminiscence:
                 New Ways of Working with Older Adults</u>.
                 New York: Haworth Press, 1984.

             Koch, Kenneth. <u>I Never Told Anybody</u>. New
                 York: Random House, 1977. Koch, a
                 poet, taught poetry writing to senior
                 adults.

             Weisberg, Naida, and Wilder, Rosilyn, eds.
                 <u>Creative Arts with Older Adults: A
                 Sourcebook</u>. New York: Human Sciences
                 Press, 1985.

             For a sample of first poems written by women
             whose average age was seventy-five years,
             you can request the little book <u>Flowering
             Moments</u> from the State of Rhode Island
             Department of Elder Affairs, State House,

Providence, Rhode Island 02803. These poems were written during a one-session poetry workshop conducted by Ruth Jacobs in 1983 in Warwick, Rhode Island.

A book of poems from the Senior Citizens' Poetry Project conducted by Steven Ratiner in Cambridge, Massachusetts, Even Now I Can Hear It, is available form the Cambridge Community Schools, Department of Human Service Programs, City Hall, Cambridge, Massachusetts 02138.

Poems from the Inside, a collection of poetry edited by Willa Schneberg and Ireta Zaretsky, is available from the Hebrew Rehabilitation Center, 1200 Centre Street, West Roxbury, Massachusetts 02132.

Examples of journal-keeping can be found in the Journal of Journals, sponsored by the Rhode Island Women's Journal Writing Collective, 141 Elton Street, Providence, Rhode Island 02906. In addition, Elizabeth G. Vining's journal, Being Seventy: The Measure of a Year (New York: Viking Press, 1978), records her experiences during the year she was seventy.

Both poems and prose by older women can be found in the magazine Broomstick, published at 3543 18th Street, San Francisco, California 94110.

SESSION 7:   TRANSFORMING AND SHARING OUR LIVES THROUGH CREATIVE EXPRESSION

In this session, the women in your group will be writing poems, keeping journals, or exploring other forms of creative expression. The aim is to enhance the women's self-esteem and to show them that, as they age, they can begin or continue to express themselves creatively. Communicating our feelings to those around us through art can be ego-enhancing, making us feel valuable and unique. In one another, the women in the group have an encouraging and responsive audience. So they may want to share their talents, some of which were hidden earlier in life because of the demands of families or work.

1.   Exploring Oral and Visual Expression

Although much of this session focuses on written expression, you may have a group of women whose writing skills are limited or who are inhibited about writing. Thus it might be necessary to utilize other forms of artistic communication. For example, you could ask the group to draw or paint scenes from important events in their lives and then tell the others about these events. Provide inexpensive newsprint paper, crayons, colored felt-tip pens, or broad-tip markers for this exercise. You can allay participants' fears by explaining that no special artistic ability is required. Emphasize that they should simply draw what they can remember of a significant event. After the women have completed their drawings, go around the circle and ask each person to describe and explain one of her works.

Music, dance, and drama can also provide means of self-expression. Some ethnic groups have very strong oral traditions and the women in your workshop may enjoy sharing folktales, stories, songs, or chants that they can remember and recite. Those who were immigrants might like to tell stories of the "old country." Some women may want to teach the others ethnic or other dances or to demonstrate folk dances. Other women may invent stories.

Even telling jokes can use the dramatic skills of the women. Sometimes stories and jokes provide an outlet for sexual feelings. Previously quiet women may open up with the opportunity to tell jokes and stories.

Another technique for encouraging oral expression is to tell a group story. Have the first woman in the circle provide the first sentence or two of a story. Go around the circle, asking each woman to add a sentence or two. A group poem could be created in the same way. Provide a cue phrase that each woman completes. For example, you might say, "Our group is..." and have each person complete the sentence with a word or several phrases. You could do the same thing with a holiday or season of the year, asking participants to complete the phrase "Christmas is..." or "Spring is..." Similarly, you could ask each person to create an image based on a color, such as "Yellow is a morning filled with hope" or "Red is the blood that binds us together." Then list all the lines about the common theme on a blackboard or large sheets of paper and you will have a group poem. (This technique is a good icebreaker, and you might want to use it initially even if your group is capable of writing.)

Handwork and crafts also provide creative outlets. You could ask the women to share samples of their craft or needlework and instructions for doing it.

Even though some women in the group may have limited language skills, you may wish to try to involve them in "writing" exercises as well. See Laura Fox's chapter on conducting writing workshops for both literate and illiterate adults in Creative Arts with Older Adults for useful suggestions. For example, women can dictate their thoughts to you or others to write down. Women for whom English is a second language might prefer to write in their native language. Another device for involving people who cannot or do not write very much is to use a tape recorder. This allows them to express their thoughts fluently by recording and then playing back their words.

2. Sharing Poems Brought in by Participants

Remind the group that at the end of the last session, you asked them to bring poetry by themselves or others which they would like to share. Ask those who brought poems to read them aloud. You might encourage the group to learn about minority women writers by reading from the work of black poets, such as Gwendolyn Brooks and Nikki Giovanni, or the work of native American, Hispanic, and Asian-American women.

3. List Poems

After sharing poems brought in by workshop members, you can suggest that everyone has lots of poems within herself. Point out that many of us learned to hate poetry by having to memorize poems in school or by having to read and analyze poems we may have disliked or found meaningless. Explain that poems do not have to be difficult, obscure, or contain rhymes as we may have been taught years ago. Poems simply are ways of sharing our feelings, memories, and insights.

Remind the group that they heard a poetic drama at the last session, and that the poems by those who played Mary, Virginia, Elizabeth, and Dora in the play were quite straightforward expressions of feelings and thoughts. Reread for them Elizabeth's poem about being seventy years of age and Dora's poem about being in her eighties. Explain that these are both list poems, in which the characters list what it is like to be their ages. A third example of a list poem is Mary's poem from the play, which begins with the line "I have learned" and tells all the ways she learned to manage in the city.

The examples that you have read are rather long list poems, but list poems can also be very short, even as brief as four lines. For example, read to the group the following poem by the author of this manual:

>   Maternal Heritage
>
>   From my mother
>   the love of poems
>   and violets.
>
>   From my grandmother
>   giving when
>   there was little left
>   to give.

If you have several women in the group who are in their sixties, you might read to them a list poem about being sixty, also by the author of this manual.

Becoming Sixty

There were terror and anger
at coming into sixty.
Would I give birth
only to my old age?

Now near sixty-one
I count the gifts
that sixty gave.

A book flowed from my life
to those who needed it
and love flowed back to me.

In a yard that had seemed full
I found space for another garden.
I took my aloneness to worship meeting
and my outstretched palms were filled.

I walked further along the beach
swam longer in more sacred places
danced the spiral dance
reclaimed daisies for women
in my ritual for a precious friend
and received poet's wine
from a new friend who came
in the evening of my need.*

Now ask the participants to "live dangerously" and to
write a list poem. It can be about anything they like.
However, the following are suggestions for topics, if
needed.

1. List good things about being your age.

2. List bad things about being your age. (Items one
    and two can be combined into one poem.)

3. List what you received from your mother, your
    grandmother, or another important person in your
    life.

---

*This poem was published in <u>Friendly Woman</u>, Volume 7
(April 1986), page 12. <u>Friendly Woman</u> is a Quaker
magazine.

4. List things you love to do.

5. List things you hate to do.

6. List some pleasant memories. The first line could
    be "I remember..." or "I can still see..." or "I
    can still hear..."

7. List some sad memories. (Again, items six and
    seven can be combined or separate.)

8. List things you want to do.

9. List what you like about someone.

List the nine poem ideas on a blackboard or on a big piece
of paper taped to the wall. Or hand out lists of the nine
poem ideas plus any you want to add. For example, if a
holiday is coming, you might suggest a list poem or any
other kind of poem about the holiday. If working with a
blackboard, flip chart, or taped sheets of paper, you may
want to add poem ideas the group suggests.

Tell the group that they will have fifteen minutes to
write a poem. Explain that the poems will be first drafts
that they may want to polish later, but you hope they will
be willing to read their rough poems aloud. As always,
explain that anyone who does not want to share may pass.
Say that if anyone would like her poem read but would
prefer not to do it herself, you will be glad to read it,
either giving her name or not, as the author prefers.
Also note that if anyone finishes before the fifteen
minutes are up, she can start a second poem of any sort
she likes.

Then give the group fifteen minutes in which to write.
Feel free to extend the time a bit if several women need a
few minutes more.

When the writing period is up, ask those who would rather
not read their own poems to give them to you, indicating
whether you should give their names by writing "anonymous"
or their names on the sheets. As an icebreaker, read your
poem or ask for a volunteer to read first. Then go around
the circle. After each poem, allow a few minutes for
expressions of appreciation but do not get involved in
criticism. Suggest that if anyone has a suggestion for
improving any poem, she can speak privately to the person

who wrote it. Remind the group that many people may be
writing their first poems and not to expect polished
efforts in such a short time.

After you have gone around the circle once, ask if anyone
who did not read a poem the first time would now like to
do so. Often a woman may think her poem is not good
enough to read initially, but gains courage after she
hears the work of other beginners. Then read the poems
written by those who did not want to read their own work
aloud.

Probably some very meaningful poems will emerge from this
process. The reading may elicit some tears as well as
laughter, but remember that sharing both sad and pleasant
feelings can be beneficial.

Participants may want copies of the poems written during
the session. If so, ask for a volunteer to type and copy
them for the next meeting.

If the list poem exercise generated enthusiasm, encourage
the women to write poems at home and to bring them to
share at future sessions. Remind the group that writing
is a wonderful way to express both positive and negative
feelings.

4. Journals

Another way to record one's feelings is by keeping a
journal. Many people keep journals in order to express
their thoughts and experiences and this can be a valuable
process. The writer can describe and analyze what is
going on inside of her. Writing things down often helps
us to think them out. Journals also can help us to see
and remember the continuity in our lives as we read and
reread the journals.

Moreover, much of women's experience has not been recorded
in standard history books but is now being recovered by
scholars from women's journals and diaries. These show
researchers what life was like for our foremothers. Many
women's journals are now valued documents in special
libraries, such as the Schlesinger Library at Radcliffe
College in Cambridge, Massachusetts, which collects
materials having to do with women. Journals also are
treasured by descendants because they contain important
family and community history. Interest in journals has

increased to the point that there is now a journal of journal entries. (This is the <u>Journal of Journals</u> listed in the reading section of the outline.)

As an example of a journal entry, read the following excerpt from the journal of a seventy-five-year-old black woman who was in a Surviving and Thriving workshop:

> What a long way I have come from Lynchburg, Virginia, where I was one of ten children and very poor. It seems only yesterday but now I am a grandmother of eleven and living in Boston. I am living by myself for the first time in my life and I love it. I can truly say I am happy, very happy. Yesterday I played the piano, danced by myself to the radio for exercise, watched the basketball game on television because I am an avid sports fan, and went to a meeting at night at my church. I love to go to church--something that happens there just lifts me up. People are so friendly. They care about you. The minister always has a good word for me and he did last night. I don't ever feel lonely. God has been good to me.

You could also read aloud a section from the journal of Elizabeth Vining. She kept a journal daily during the seventieth year of her life. Her journal has been published as <u>Being Seventy: The Measure of a Year</u>, and it is available in most libraries. (See the reading suggestions for bibliographic information.)

Suggest to the group that retrospective accounts of their lives or journal entries would be valuable to their families and to scholars. Of course, they do not have to do this unless they are interested. Journal entries can be done on tape recorders too.

If there is enough time left in this session, ask the women to write a first journal entry. Tell them they can write about anything they want. But if they need suggestions, they could write about the group itself, what yesterday was like for them, or something in the more distant past. Or they could write about things in their lives for which they are thankful or about things they would like to change.

Then ask each woman who is willing to read a few of the lines she has written. If there is not enough time to do this during the session, suggest that the participants write journal entries at home. If you wish, mention that short selections from written or taped journals can be heard at future sessions. If women do bring in selections, make time for these, as you should for new poems brought in. If time is short, you can copy and distribute writings instead of having them read aloud.

In general, be careful to give equal attention to the more polished writers and those whose work is less sophisticated. If you discover something that is publishable, speak to the writer privately. If your workshop proves to be full of writers, perhaps their poetry or journal entries could be shared with students or others in the community.

On occasion the writing exercises are so popular that women decide to start groups where they discuss ongoing writings. This also provides a way to continue group activity after the workshop ends. If only a few women are interested in a writers' group, check with your public library to find out if there are any writers' groups in your community. Or your local senior center might sponsor one.

Some participants may be interested in taking literature or creative writing courses. Public colleges in many states waive or reduce tuition for those over sixty or sixty-five years of age who wish to take courses. Some private colleges also do this. In addition, Elder Hostels may have literature courses. (Elder Hostels provide live-in stays at colleges and other places around the country, and even abroad, for persons over age sixty. Courses, recreation, food, and lodging are packaged at a reasonable cost. For information about Elder Hostel programs, write them at 80 Boylston Street, Suite 400, Boston, Massachusetts 02116.) Adult education programs or community centers may also offer creative writing courses.

If someone in your group is interested in trying to publish her writings, she can try any of numerous outlets. Local newspapers often print poems by residents. Church bulletins and ethnic magazines sometimes publish creative writing, as do magazines aimed at older readers.

Modern Maturity, published by the American Association of Retired Persons, has a page of poems in most issues. The editorial address of Modern Maturity is 215 Long Beach Boulevard, Long Beach, California 90801.

Broomstick, a magazine "By, For and About Women Over Forty," is published bimonthly from 3543 18th Street, San Francisco, California 94110. This journal accepts contributions only from women over forty years of age. Many authors are first-time writers. Broomstick prints poems and journal-type pieces.

Another magazine that prints writings by older persons is December Rose, published quarterly from 255 South Hill Street, Los Angeles, California 90012. An article by Isabelle Goldsmith, a poet, from the winter 1984 issue is reproduced here as an optional handout. Next to the article is a column with information on how to submit writings to the magazine.

5. Questions about Sexuality and Family Life

Some of the poems and journal entries written during this session may have been about relatives and some may have expressed sexual feelings. Either after these are read or at the end of the session, announce that the next session will cover family relations and sexuality. Ask participants to think about these topics and bring in any questions they may have in written form, if they feel they will not be able to ask them publicly. Remind them they can also use the questionnaire forms provided in Session Five to present problems.

6. Closing Ritual

Don't forget some kind of ending ritual.

Love Brings Young, Old to Common Ground

By Isabelle Goldsmith

In old age, make the most of less of life.

Go at it with a bounce and you will help unburden the younger generation, who now may only regard you as old. Give youth a tender embrace, a cheerful smile. Good spirits are contagious. Be witty, not peeved. Develop a sense of humor instead of feeling sorry for yourself.

This will lift the veil of separation and the young will welcome you into their world. You will go back in years and feel young at heart, standing with them on common ground regardless of age difference.

The young intuitively sense your appeal. In their eyes, you rise above the average. You have what they have yet to get hold of—a blossoming wisdom.

How can I instill in their minds a fragment of this wisdom's essence? Will they listen? Will they ask for it? Life's preparedness does not work that way. God alone shows the way.

While forging through life on my own, I searched for the "impossible" and the possible emerged. I graduated from the school of life with the wisdom to carry on and impart to others.

Take it from someone who was 92 in August. I say: Be not disheartened. It is never too late to put across a message that lives after you.

Think of yourself as an invisible star moving in the same orbit with all the brilliant stars who have that God-given command of their wisdom to thwart the negative, opposing forces that seek to throw them off balance, and never can.

Consider these three principles:

1. Keep your mind off yourself.

2. Reach the hearts of others. Decipher what is secreted there. Then, in your own way answer their silent cries to release their hearts and souls.

3. Play gently and kindly on human emotions and you will perform one of those little wonders that attract the young to you without asking.

Plant the seeds of wisdom in the garden of your heart and soul where they can take root. Let God be in all your moves as you let these seeds grow.

Having this wisdom at your command brings humanity close to you to be wanted, needed and loved. Such closeness is one of life's great experiences. For when love takes over, it makes out of both your worlds, one world. For this, we give thanks to God.

December Rose encourages your submissions

The *December Rose* Magazine welcomes submissions in fiction and nonfiction writing, poetry, photography, music and all forms of art.

In addition, we are interested in stories about older people whose creative lifestyles exemplify the art of living.

Ideas and letters to the editor will be accepted without the submission form.

To submit an article or artwork, contact the December Rose Association, 255 S. Hill St., #407, Los Angeles, Calif. 90012—or call (213) 617-7002—for an official submission form.

This form must be accompanied by a brief biography of the artist or author, a 5 × 7 or 8 × 10 black-and-white photograph of the artist/author and a 35 mm slide or glossy photo of the artwork to be considered. (These may or may not be used for publication purposes.)

Manuscripts may be typed or handwritten. The editors reserve the right to edit the material and use it in any form. The December Rose Association is not responsible for return of unsolicited materials.

Only original material (no reprints) will be considered.

From <u>December Rose</u>, Winter 1984. Used with persmission.

SESSION 8

SEXUALITY AND FAMILY RELATIONS

BRIEF OUTLINE

OBJECTIVES: To help women feel more comfortable with their sexuality or celibacy.
To provide information, support, and ideas about family relationships.

MATERIALS: Index cards, blackboard, or large sheets of paper on the wall.

PROCEDURES: 1. Optional: pass out list of local resources if you have made one.
2. Discuss anonymous questionnaire cases on sexuality and written "homework" questions.
3. Pass out and discuss An Alphabet of Ways of Expressing Sexuality for Older Women. Or have women write on index cards how they express sexuality. Share and discuss these comments.
4. Break into small groups in order to discuss family issues. Also handle family questionnaire cases.
5. Brainstorm about common problems and their solutions.
6. Pass out and discuss Rules for Generational Relationships.
7. Closing ritual.

HANDOUTS: An Alphabet of Ways of Expressing Sexuality for Older Women
Rules for Generational Relationships
Optional: List of local resources
Poems written by participants in Session Seven, if you had these recorded and copied.

READING: 1. Suggestions for further reading on sexuality:

Boston Women's Health Book Collective. <u>Our Bodies, Ourselves: A Book by and for Women</u>. New York: Simon & Schuster, 1984.

Brecher, Edward M., and the Editors of Consumers Union. <u>Love, Sex and Aging</u>. Boston: Little Brown, 1984.

Butler, Robert, and Lewis, Myrna. <u>Love and Sex After Sixty: A Guide for Men and Women in Their Later Years</u>. New York: Harper & Row, 1976.

"Sexuality in Later Life," an issue of the <u>Journal of Geriatric Psychiatry</u> (Volume XVII, Number 2, 1984), has helpful information in it. This journal is available from International Universities Press, Inc., 315 Fifth Avenue, New York, New York 10016. It can also be found in university and hospital libraries.

<u>Growing Older, Getting Better</u> by Jane Porcino, recommended earlier, has a chapter entitled "Sexuality and Intimacy as We Age" and includes a list of resources. This book also has a chapter and resources on family matters.

2. Two books on grandparenting are:

Dodson, Fitzhugh, and Reuban, Paula. <u>How to Grandparent</u>. New York: Harper & Row, 1981.

Kornhaber, Arthur, and Woodward, Kenneth. <u>Grandparents/Grandchildren: The Vital Connection</u>. New York: Doubleday, 1981.

<u>The Journal of Geriatric Psychiatry</u> (Volume 19, Number 1, 1986) is a special issue on grandparenting.

3. Other family relationships:

Your public library will have plenty of advice books about family matters.

On the problems faced by adults who care for aging parents, see:

Goodman, Jane Goz. <u>Aging Parents: Whose Responsibility?</u> Milwaukee: Family Service America, 1980.

Silverstone, Barbara, and Hynan, Helen Kandel. <u>You and Your Aging Parents</u>. New York: Pantheon, 1976.

SESSION 8:   SEXUALITY AND FAMILY RELATIONS

Issues related to sexuality and family life probably have
surfaced already during the course of previous sessions.
Sexual or family problems may have been presented on the
anonymous questionnaires. Intimacy needs may have been
listed and discussed in Session Three during the problem
identification exercise, and in Session Four, certain
rules and advice submitted by the women probably dealt
with family relations and perhaps with sexuality. In
addition, sexuality issues were raised in the play
presented during Session Six and very likely were noted in
the discussion afterward.

If you, as leader, feel uncomfortable with the topic, you
may decide to bring in an expert for the sexuality
session. However, assuming that you will lead the session
yourself, keep in mind that you will be covering
particularly sensitive issues. Be especially careful of
the need for privacy and sensitive to feelings of
discomfort or embarrassment. Older women are often
inhibited about discussing intimate issues. They may have
misinformation left over from their early lives, when
sexual information was less available, myths more
prevalent, and societal values different regarding family
and intimate relationships.

As always, adapt the suggestions in the manual to the
needs of the women in your group. Obviously, the issues
and problems are different for married women than they are
for those who are widowed, divorced, never married, or
lesbian. In leading this session, consider the
composition of your group, the degree of rapport
established among the women, and their cultural and
religious backgrounds.

Sexuality and family relations are big topics.
Suggestions for handling both are presented here in a
single session, but you might want to plan two separate
sessions instead.

1.   Local Resources

If you do not have an outside expert at your session on
sexuality and family matters and this is not an area of

special expertise for you, prepare a list of local resources with the names of agencies and professionals in your area who offer help with serious problems of sexual dysfunction or of family disturbance. Distribute this resource list at the beginning of the session to avoid jeopardizing anyone's sense of privacy by being singled out for referral.

Emphasize that participants should not expect answers to very complicated individual problems in this session but rather advice on more general issues that affect many older women. Explain that certain questions might be more appropriate to ask physicians, psychologists, counselors, members of the clergy, or other professional health and family service workers. Urge participants to discuss especially difficult private problems with professionals.

This session focuses on problems most older women share or can relate to and that can be discussed in a group of peers. The goal is for group members to help one another with matters that do not require professional assistance but rather common sense and shared experience.

Begin with a discussion of sexuality. This topic may occupy the entire session and you can postpone the family relations discussion for another time. Conversely, if too much inhibition prevails, you can move on to family issues. In addition, some women's sexual practices are separate from family relationships and you do not want to make them uncomfortable by combining the two topics.

2. "Homework Questions" and Anonymous Questionnaires

Collect questions on sexuality and family relations that participants did at home, following last week's instructions. Give out index cards, asking the group to write comments or questions if they forgot to do so at home or just thought of them, without signing their names. When you collect the cards, divide them into sexuality and family questions as best you can, although some may overlap. Then shuffle the cards to ensure anonymity.

Next read about the sexuality cases on the anonymous questionnaires and then the sexuality questions or comments on index cards. After each one, ask the group members to give their views. Go around the circle so that everyone has a chance to speak or not, as they choose.

3. An Alphabet of Ways of Expressing Sexuality

Distribute the handout An Alphabet of Ways of Expressing
Sexuality for Older Women. This handout lists a variety
of ways women choose to express themselves sexually. It
presents a range or continuum of behavior that research
has found among older women, including adaptation to
situations of being alone or where male partners have lost
potency or sexual interest. Thus the "Alphabet" helps
women to eradicate uncertainty or guilt about their own
practices.

The "Alphabet" also may reassure your group that many
women do, in fact, continue to be interested in sex as
they grow older. Research has shown that loss of sexual
interest occurs more often for older men than older
women. Also, because many women are younger than their
spouses and live longer, they are more apt to lose their
partners in later life. Moreover, according to
researchers, it is easier for an older man to find a
female partner than for an older woman to find a male
partner because of the longevity of women and the
preference of men for younger partners.

The "Alphabet" should provide the basis for a frank
discussion of sexual practices. But do not be surprised
or upset if you have a reticent group. Provide the
opportunity for them to talk but accept shyness also. The
handout may be helpful to people even if they do not say
anything.

An alternative approach is to delay distributing the
"Alphabet" handout. Instead, distribute index cards and
ask the women to respond to the question: "What do you do
about your sexual feelings?" Remind them not to sign
their names. Collect these cards. Shuffle them, pass
them around, and have everyone read one. This technique
works better with a bigger group, as there will be a
greater variety of responses. After reading these cards,
distribute the "Alphabet" handout as well.

4. Family Problems

When and if the sexuality discussion tapers off, move to
family relationships. Ask how many of the women have a
perfect relationship all the time with every one of their
children and relatives. There will probably be no hands

raised. This should reassure group members that they are
not alone in having tensions or difficulties. People
often assume that things are perfect for everyone else and
it is comforting to know that others have similar problems.

Divide into groups of four (or three or five, whatever is
convenient) to talk about problems with children,
husbands, or other relatives. Lifelong singles may want
to talk about relationships with their siblings or life
partners who are not spouses; lesbian women might want to
talk about relationships with lovers. Have each group
designate a "secretary" to report back to the group as a
whole what was discussed. Give the groups twenty minutes
and ask that each woman talk for five minutes about her
family issues. Of course, any woman can opt out of
talking. You may want to designate a timer in each group
to announce when a speaker's five minutes are up. Or you
may want to keep time yourself, calling out "four minutes"
and then "five minutes and time to switch to the next
person." If you are devoting a whole session to family
issues, you might want to increase the amount of time
given to each speaker.

At the end of the small group discussions, see if more
time is needed. Allow another five minutes or so if the
groups feel they need more time to finish. Then have the
"secretaries" report about the problems and solutions that
emerged in each group. Write these on a blackboard or
paper on the wall.

5. Brainstorming

Ask the group to brainstorm about possible solutions to
the common problems that have emerged. Some good ideas
will probably come from the group, and even if not all
problems are solved, it can be comforting for participants
to see that others have similar problems. For example,
widows often find family and friends drifting away from
them after the immediate crisis of losing a husband.
Married women may have problems with spouses. Some women
may feel neglected by their children. Another common
concern is how to treat adult children and grandchildren.

Those women who live with or care for aging parents may
have many questions and concerns. Some of the women in
the group who are sixty or seventy years of age may be
caretakers for or at least have parents who are in their
eighties and nineties. If relationships with elderly

parents are a significant issue for your participants, you
may want to use exercises and information from the manual
Aging Parents: Whose Responsibility? by Jane Goz Goodman
cited in the reading list for this session. Or, if you
have the appropriate background to do so, you can plan a
follow-up workshop for caretakers of elderly parents using
that manual.

After the brainstorming process is concluded, read and
discuss family problems raised on the index cards and
anonymous questionnaires, if you have reserved some of
these for the session. Use the same discussion techniques
as for the sexuality questions and cases; go around the
circle, asking each participant to comment or not, as she
chooses.

6. Rules for Generational Relationships

Distribute the second handout for this session, the Rules
for Generational Relationships. Note that these rules
offer suggestions for dealing with younger and older
family members.

7. Closing Ritual

Don't forget a closing ritual.

AN ALPHABET OF WAYS OF EXPRESSING SEXUALITY FOR OLDER WOMEN

There are only twenty-six letters in the alphabet; thus only twenty-six styles of sexual expression are given here. Actually, there are many more kinds of sexual expression and this alphabet is only a sampler of possibilities. You may not find yourself or your particular style here. You might find that you combine aspects of several of the styles presented. Each woman's style is presented very briefly and more could be said about each of them.

ANNE, who is married, has sexual intercourse with her husband, although not as frequently as in earlier years. They enjoy their sexual activity very much. Anne and her husband have a longer period of foreplay than they did formerly because it takes him longer to achieve an erection. Sometimes they have oral sex, which works well for them. They asked their doctor for information about positions and techniques that are more comfortable for older people. Among these are that Anne stimulates her husband's genitals with her caresses and he stimulates her as well. Also they use a sideways position for making love. Anne uses mineral oil as a clitoral and vaginal lubricant, although her friend, Sara, uses a prescription item her doctor recommended.

BARBARA, who is single, has a male friend who generally spends one night a week at her apartment and shares her bed. She has known him for several years, having met him at the senior center shortly after his wife died. Sometimes they vacation together.

CAROL has been unable to find a male partner, although she would like to. She masturbates to relieve her sexual tension. Carol has read that about twenty-five percent of older women do so, including some whose husbands are no longer sexually active with them.

DOROTHY has been a lesbian all of her life and she continues to have a sexual relationship with the woman who has been her lifetime partner.

EVELYN, in younger years, had relationships with men. Now she meets few available men and she satisfies her sexual needs with other women.

FRIEDA is close to her women friends and shares good and bad times with them. But she does not have sexual relationships with them and would not consider this, although she finds it nice to touch and hug her women friends. They all enjoy the human warmth and comforting.

GERTRUDE never did really enjoy her sexual life. Having recently divorced, she is relieved not to be bothered with sex. She gets along very well without it. So does her friend, Glenda, a lifelong celibate who is happy with her situation.

HELEN, a widow, misses romance but has not met anyone her age who is both suitable and single. Anyway, her moral views include the conviction that sex should only be a part of marriage. She does enjoy reading novels and short stories about sexual experiences of others and likes movies that have sexual themes.

IDA, a widow, misses being touched and gets a health massage once a week. She also takes bubble baths to relax and sometimes dances alone to records.

JUDITH hopes to find a male partner. She puts ads in a singles magazine seeking a nice, respectable man of about seventy years of age, who likes quiet evenings at home. In the meantime, she masturbates.

KATHERINE attends dances. She talks and dances with men she meets there and enjoys this very much. But she goes home alone. She does not want involvement.

LILLIAN also goes to dances and enjoys dancing with men. Sometimes Lillian goes to a singles club for older adults where she meets men. When she likes a man and knows him well enough to be sure he is trustworthy, Lillian invites him home and they might have sex.

MARILYN accepts celibacy in her old age. She makes sure that she gets plenty of exercise. She loves nature and enjoys taking long walks. Marilyn keeps busy by volunteering at church and elsewhere.

NORA and her friends enjoy telling "off-color" jokes. They also talk about their past romances, having none now in their lives.

OPHELIA says her relationship with her husband was wonderful and nobody will ever take his place. She has two cats to which she gives lots of affection. Ophelia keeps busy with lots of hobbies.

PRISCILLA plays the piano whenever she gets tense. She likes romantic songs.

QUEENIE remarried recently at seventy-five years of age to an eighty-one-year-old man. "We are like kids," she says.

ROBERTA enjoys swimming at the YWCA, where she likes the intimacy of the locker room. Women are uninhibited there and it is okay to be nude--wrinkles, bulges, and all. Now single, she revels in the freedom from the many responsibilities that she had in her marriage.

SALLY meets her sensual needs by eating and cooking, as well as gardening and handling beautiful flowers. She also loves fabrics and sewing. Sally enjoys children, so she babysits for the infant children of her friends and neighbors. She loves to pat babies and children and kiss their soft heads.

THELMA reads magazines and books that are very erotic, even pornographic. She laughs that she now has to hide things from her grown children, instead of the other way around as when they were adolescents at home.

UNA, who is in a nursing home, has a very close relationship with a man in the home. They kiss and touch whenever they have a chance and spend as much time together as possible. They would like the comfort of sharing a bed and wish the staff were less opposed to this.

VERA has a much older husband who is an invalid. Sexual acts are not possible for him, but she gives him lots of tender, loving care. Vera bathes her husband gently, brushes his hair, and kisses him. She finds this satisfying.

WILHEMINA worries a lot about the sexual promiscuity of young people today. She spends a lot of time at church praying for them. She tries not to think about sex herself.

XIMENA paints very romantic pictures full of lovers and flowers, and daydreams about love.

YVETTE has a husband who says he is not interested in sex anymore. Yvette has made arrangements for the two of them to get counseling at a family service agency. Yvette checked with her family doctor, who advised her that her husband has a psychological hangup about aging. Recently Yvette has read some books on the sexuality of older adults.

ZENA gets a lot of pleasure out of dressing attractively, being well groomed, and receiving compliments on her appearance. She loves using cosmetics and perfume. Zena flirts a bit with men of all ages, "harmlessly," as she says. She hopes some day "Mr. Right" will appear but in the meantime she enjoys life.

RULES FOR GENERATIONAL RELATIONSHIPS

For your adult children, grandchildren, and aging parents, the same rules apply. They are:

1. Never do anything for them they can do for themselves. This infantilizes and creates dependency and anger.

2. Never make plans for them without consulting them. Practically everyone functions better with a sense of autonomy.

3. Avoid the idealization of youth or old age. You cannot make things perfect for your children or your parents.

4. Never shortchange yourself or postpone your own living. Do not be callous but do respect your needs. Otherwise you will become resentful and it will show and poison relationships.

5. Know and use outside resources. There are community programs and good advisors for both young and old.

6. Get support from others in the same boat. You are not alone. Do not reinvent the wheel. Learn from others' experience.

7. Save something for your very old age. You do not have to sacrifice yourself to the generations behind and ahead. If not now, when?

8. Be honest. Both young and old people would rather have the truth than evasiveness. You cannot fool either.

9. Be patient with both. Youth and extreme old age are stressful in American society and both young and old are grasping for status in a society that devalues them.

10. Do not talk down to either generation. Be yourself. Do not reach for the current slang to communicate with the young and avoid talking geri-talk (demeaning simplification) to the old. In other words, respect the ability of the young and the old.

11. Try to laugh with both but not at them. Shared laughter bonds, mockery wounds.

12. Accept that values of generations change as society changes. Be as flexible as you can. Hold to your values if you wish but understand that others have different ones.

SESSION 9

FINANCIAL MANAGEMENT AND LIVING ARRANGEMENTS

BRIEF OUTLINE

OBJECTIVES: To give help in financial management.
                To explore options in housing.

MATERIALS: Index cards. Blackboard, flip chart, or
                large sheets of paper on the wall.
                Optional: brochures about local resources.

PROCEDURES: 1. You might have a financial-management
                    professional speak.
                2. Brainstorm in small groups about ways to
                    manage financially.
                3. Share group expertise on financial
                    benefits and discounts for older persons.
                4. Do exercise on what is needed to make a
                    living place a home.
                5. Prioritize housing needs and discuss
                    them in regard to available residence
                    options.
                6. Discuss shared housing.
                7. Discuss how to make homes safer for
                    older persons. Have suggestions
                    recorded and copied for next session.
                8. Optional: special exercises are
                    provided for residents of senior-citizen
                    housing or nursing homes.
                9. Closing ritual.

HANDOUTS: Optional: Brochures or information about
                           local housing resources and/or
                           financial-management assistance
                           for older persons.

READING: 1. Finances:

                Drawing on the resources of your public
                library and local senior citizens' centers

or agencies, assemble some books and pamphlets that can give participants a sense of the information available to them. Libraries also have many books on managing finances after retirement. Find out if there are courses on financial management given locally that participants can take.

Jane Porcino's Growing Older, Getting Better has a chapter on finances and list of resources. In addition, general guides such as Sylvia Porter's New Money Book for the 80s (New York: Avon, 1980) are useful. Another source of information is the American Association of Retired Persons, which has many pamphlets on financial planning. See the bibliography at the end of the manual for the address of this organization's national office.

2. Living arrangements:

Once again, Jane Porcino's book has a resource list and discussion of housing options. For individuals who are considering moving into public housing, there is an excellent 28-page pamphlet called Apartment for Rent: A Guide to Public Housing for the Elderly by Mary Kalymun, Ph.D. The pamphlet is free and it is available from Dr. Kalymun at the Department of Human Development, Counseling and Family Studies, the University of Rhode Island, Kingston, Rhode Island 02881. In fact, the booklet is useful for anyone planning an apartment change because it presents items to consider in choosing an apartment and helpful ideas for making a smooth transition.

Other information resources include:

Action for Boston Community Development. Shared Living An Individual Planning Guide. Boston: Action for Boston Community Development, 1985). This booklet is available from ABCD at 178 Tremont Street, Boston, Massachusetts 02111.

American Association of Retired Persons.
     <u>Your Home, Your Choice, a Workbook for
     Older People</u>. Washington, D.C.:
     American Association of Retired Persons,
     1985. This book is available free. The
     association's address is 1909 K Street,
     N.W., Washington, D.C. 20049.

Chellis, R. D.; Seagle, J. F., Jr.; and
     Seagle, B. M. <u>Congregate Housing for
     Older People: A Solution for the
     1980s</u>. Lexington, Massachusetts:
     Lexington Books, 1982.

Gold, Margaret. <u>The Older American's Guide
     to Housing and Living Arrangements</u>.
     Mount Vernon, New York: Institute for
     Consumer Policy Research, 1985. This
     publication is available from the
     Institute for Consumer Policy Research,
     Consumer's Union, 256 Washington Street,
     Mount Vernon, New York 10553.

Hubbard, Linda. <u>Housing Options for Older
     Adults</u>. Washington, D.C.: American
     Association of Retired Persons, 1984.
     This is available free from the American
     Association of Retired Persons, 1909 K
     Street, N.W., Washington, D.C. 20049.

<u>Journal of Housing for the Elderly</u>. This is
     a quarterly publication, available from
     the Haworth Press, 28 East 22nd Street,
     New York, New York 10010.

Lawton, M. Powell, et al. <u>Community Housing
     Choices for Older Americans</u>. New York:
     Spring Publishing Company, 1984.
     Spring's address is 200 Park Avenue
     South, New York, New York 10003.

Parker, Rosetta. <u>Housing for the Elderly:
     The Handbook for Managers</u>. Chicago:
     Institute of Real Estate Management,
     1984. This book is available from the
     National Association of Realtors, 430
     North Michigan Avenue, Chicago, Illinois
     60611.

SESSION 9:   FINANCIAL MANAGEMENT AND LIVING ARRANGEMENTS

1. Outside Speakers

Because of the complexity of financial management and
housing issues for older adults, you may decide to invite
experts to handle these two topics. If you do, be sure to
choose someone who does not have a particular product or
service to sell. Instead you need a speaker who can
present an unbiased, balanced body of information.

If you choose to lead this session yourself, remember that
many widows or divorced women left financial management to
their husbands and need basic information on how to
balance a checkbook, deal with banks, taxes, investment,
estate planning, budgeting, and real estate. Whole
courses are devoted to financial management for older
adults. One cannot expect to cover all the issues in half
of one session, or even an entire session. Of course, you
might decide to cover financial management and living
arrangements in two separate sessions. Even so, real
coverage of the financial management issues would require
a multisession workshop devoted only to finances and led
by an expert in the field.

This session is thus limited to basic matters. The
content will vary according to the financial status of
your participants. The issues that concern an affluent
group are different from what concerns women who live on
Social Security or Supplemental Security Income. Minority
women, in particular, are apt to suffer financial
hardships. Discussing finances with women from varied
economic strata is difficult and perhaps unrealistic.

Check around to see what resources are available in your
community for helping women who need assistance with
financial management or who need financial aid
themselves. Provide a list of local resources, if
possible.

2. Brainstorming on Financial Management

By swapping ideas on money matters you can accomplish a
good deal within the group. Something similar was done in
Session Five when the group brainstormed about inexpensive

recreation and thrift shops. Devote part of this session
to going around the circle, asking the group members to
share ideas on how they survive or thrive economically.

Participants may be reluctant to talk about how much money
they have or spend. In the United States, many people
feel financial issues are even more private than sexual
ones. Some are afraid to ask financial questions for fear
they will be thought stupid. So, in addition to going
around the circle, you can use the technique of anonymous
index cards to allow the women to ask questions and share
information.

Any group of older women will have many good ideas about
how to cut expenses. Establish a supportive atmosphere by
telling the group not to be embarrassed to share any
suggestion, simple or funny as it may seem, for it may
help someone else. Either go around the circle for
contributions, or divide the women into groups of four, as
in previous sessions, and have the small-group secretaries
report. Useful information should emerge that will be
handy in day-to-day management.

3. Share Information About Special Benefits for Older
    Persons

Older women, as a group, are the poorest people in the
United States, so this session may yield many stories of
struggle. You, or some of the participants, may know of
free or low-cost resources to which older individuals are
entitled. These include senior-citizens' discounts, free
admissions, subsidized rent, food stamps, food
distribution, free clinics, and senior-citizens' outings.
Federal parks and many state parks offer free admission to
those older than sixty-five. Your group members should be
encouraged to use these benefits and discounts.
Unfortunately, many older persons think it is accepting
"charity" to take things to which they are really
entitled. Emphasize that older people who worked hard all
their lives frequently are victims of inflation. They
deserve to enjoy whatever benefits the government,
community agencies, or businesses offer senior citizens.
In addition, many benefits go unclaimed because people do
not know about them or understand the system.

Some group members may be losing out on "freebies" and
opportunities because they refuse to identify themselves
as senior citizens; they don't like to tell their ages.

Do a little good-natured kidding about this. Point out what they are losing. Some members of your group are likely to tell about the benefits obtained from carrying a senior card and acknowledging their ages.

4. <u>Housing</u>

For most older persons, as for many Americans, housing is the most expensive item in the budget. In the past, as a rule, people spent one-fourth of their incomes for housing. Now it costs many people much more than that. So housing and financial management are interrelated topics.

Many older women see no alternative to living alone, but many other possible living arrangements exist. These include living in a single-family house, apartment, condominium, or mobile home. Home-sharing with relatives or with others is another possibility. For example, an older woman could occupy a special apartment attached to a larger house in which family or friends live. Another alternative is congregate housing--common living and dining rooms for residents who have individual or shared bedrooms. Retirement and life-care communities offer yet another kind of living environment. Residential hotels, YWCAs, and other group residences such as homes for the elderly, nursing homes, and boarding houses should also be considered. Many different agencies--governmental, civic, private, religious, and ethnic--sponsor housing for the elderly and innovative forms of group housing are being developed. See the reading list for more information on housing options.

To stimulate thinking on housing alternatives, start with a group brainstorming exercise. Ask the participants for a list of what is needed to make a living place into a home. Write the answers on a blackboard, flip chart, or large sheets of paper on the wall. Tell the women to call out things such as a place to sleep, telephone, food, television, near transportation, plants, privacy, pets, comfortable chairs, view, neighbors, and affordability. Keep asking for more until you get a very long list that includes everyone's needs and wants. Probably someone in your group will say "people." If not, you could add people to the list yourself. This seems an obvious thing but many older women have become reconciled to living alone or see no alternative. Statistics show that forty-five percent of women over sixty-five years of age live alone.

5. Prioritize Housing Needs

After completing the above list, have the group vote on
which items are absolutely indispensable. Star these.
Then vote on which items are high priorities but not
absolutely essential. Check those. The rest of the items
are clearly desirable but probably people could manage
without them if other things compensated.

Then ask the group what kind of housing older women can
and do live in. Brainstorm a list of possible living
arrangements. This should include items like one's own
single-family home, apartment, apartment in housing for
the elderly, shared housing with one person, shared
apartment with one person, nursing home, rest home, home
for the elderly, mobile home, condominium, room in someone
else's home, living with children, residential hotel,
living with other relatives, living in a group, and living
at the YWCA. Ask if there is anything else.

Next, bring back the list of housing priorities. Ask the
group to consider how many of the essential and
high-priority items on that list are provided by each kind
of possible living arrangement. Encourage discussion
about what various modes of living offer.

6. Shared Housing

Point out that many women who are alone have found new
life-styles living with others in group arrangements that
provide both private and communal space. Many large older
homes can be shared by women who were having trouble
managing alone. Shared living arrangements can have many
social and financial benefits, as well as providing a
safer environment.

Ask the participants to suggest ways in which people who
have difficulty living alone could share homes.
Brainstorm on this. For example, are there any colleges
or schools nearby? Might students, faculty, or staff need
off-campus housing and be willing to pay and/or do chores
in return for living space?

Some women may begin to see the advantages of congregate
living as well as other housing alternatives. If you can
provide information about local housing programs, do so.
However, the point of this discussion is not to persuade
anyone to change her life-style, only to make people aware

of the alternatives. Very likely the women in your
workshop will themselves have different kinds of housing
arrangements and can get ideas from one another.

7. Home Safety

Many accidents happen to older people in their own homes.
Ask the group to list methods by which homes could be made
safer. These could include removing scatter rugs and long
electric cords upon which people often trip, getting a
guard rail and rubber treads for the bathtub, installing
an emergency alarm system for those who live alone, not
smoking in bed, becoming part of a mutual checkup system
of daily telephone calls, putting treads and railings on
staircases, not wearing loose slippers in the house, and
so forth. Group discussion should yield many good
suggestions. If your group expresses sufficient interest,
ask someone to record the safety ideas and copy them to
distribute at the next session.

8. Exercises for Groups in Senior-Citizens' Housing or
    Nursing Homes

If the members of the workshop all live in an
elderly-housing complex where everyone has much the same
living arrangement, alter the session to meet their
needs. Focus on the safety questions mentioned above.
Discuss issues relevant to their situation, such as how to
encourage good relations among residents in the housing
project, how to deal with the management, and problem
neighbors. Identify concerns by having people list the
situations or problems in their complex about which they
would like to talk. This could be done in several ways:
by going around the circle, by breaking into small
discussion groups, or by writing items for discussion on
index cards, if there are sensitive issues to be addressed.

If you are working with a group in a nursing home or other
long-term care facility, ask the residents to think and
talk about how they can help improve their living
situation. What are their needs in this regard and how
can those needs be met? Ask what they can do collectively
to support and contribute to this process. For example,
you might have them draw up a joint letter to present to
the management explaining what is unsatisfactory about the
facility and detailing what could be done to make it more
comfortable. Or the participants could rehearse for a
meeting with management.

An organization called LIFE (Life Is For Everyone) might be a helpful resource in working with nursing-home residents. LIFE has chapters in many long-term care facilities and the organization helps residents to have a sense of autonomy, dignity, and community. The founder of this organization, social worker Edward Alessi, can be contacted at the Bedford Veterans' Administration Hospital, Bedford, Massachusetts.

9. <u>Closing Ritual</u>

As usual, provide a nice closing ceremony.

SESSION 10

HEALTH MAINTENANCE AND MEDICAL CARE

BRIEF OUTLINE

OBJECTIVES: To share wisdom about health maintenance.
To prepare older women to cope with health care providers.

MATERIALS: Blackboard, flip chart, or large sheets of paper on the wall. A clock or watch to pass. Paper and pens or pencils if you wish to query the women on their health concerns.

PROCEDURES:
1. Share information about health-maintenance practices.
2. Discuss and/or distribute list of good health practices.
3. Discussion of ways to ensure good nutrition.
4. Have "I Deserve" ceremony after which each person agrees to do one new healthy thing for herself.
5. Share mental-health ideas.
6. Discussion of relationships with health-care providers. Distribute and discuss list of strategies for dealing with medical professionals.
7. Role playing.
8. Remind the group that only two more sessions remain.
9. Close with an exercise.

HANDOUTS: List of Suggestions on Health
Older Women's Strategies for Dealing with Health Care Professionals
Optional: Home safety tips from previous session, if you had them recorded and copied.
Free pamphlets on health maintenance.

READING: Jane Porcino's <u>Growing Older, Getting Better</u>
has chapters on topics such as menopause,
fitness, osteoporosis, common health
problems of older women, addictions, and
economic concerns. See also <u>Our Bodies,</u>
<u>Ourselves</u> by the Boston Women's Health Book
Collective (cited in the outline for Session
Eight) for much useful information.

Free pamphlets on health topics are
available from the American Association of
Retired Persons. This organization will
provide a list of all their pamphlets upon
request. For this session, you may wish to
obtain the following:

<u>The Prudent Patient, How to Get the Most</u>
<u>for Your Health Care Dollar</u>

<u>Cut the Cost Keep the Care: New Action</u>
<u>Steps for 1985-86</u>

<u>Medicare and Health Insurance for Older</u>
<u>People</u>

<u>Sodium: Facts for Older Citizens</u>

<u>Organizing Educational Seminars</u>
(Displays and slides are available.)

<u>Prescription for Action</u>

<u>Have You Heard</u>?

<u>Eating for Good Health</u>

<u>Healthy Questions</u>

<u>Pep Up Your Life: A Fitness Exercise</u>
<u>Book for Seniors</u>

<u>Using Medicines Wisely</u>

<u>More Health for Your Dollars: An Older</u>
<u>Person's Guide to HMO's</u>

<u>A Handbook about Care in the Home</u>

Government and private agencies also publish
leaflets and booklets on health topics for
older persons. A Guide to Medical Self-Care
and Self-Help Groups for the Elderly, a 1980
publication of the National Institute on
Aging, is available from the Superintendent
of Documents, U.S. Government Printing
Office, Washington, D.C. 20402.

The Gray Panthers' position paper, An Apple
a Day Won't Do It, is available from their
national office. Your public library will
be a good source of information about how
additional pamphlets can be obtained from
state and municipal agencies.

SESSION 10: HEALTH MAINTENANCE AND MEDICAL CARE

The first half of this session focuses on preventive
health care. This includes nutrition, exercise, and
mental health. The second part of the session deals with
older women's relationships with health-care providers.
At the start of this session, you could ask the women to
write anonymously and briefly what their health concerns
are. If you read aloud these concerns, some may feel
relief in knowing that others have health problems similar
to their own. This also sets the stage for discussion.

1. Share Information About Good Health Practices

Go around the circle, asking each woman to give her ideas
about what constitute good health maintenance practices.
Remind participants to mention their ordinary routines or
habits as these may be helpful to others. If you have
women from different ethnic backgrounds in your workshop,
encourage them to share information about such matters as
cultural practices, customs, and cooking that contribute
to good health. Pass the clock or watch around the circle
and limit each speaker to five or ten minutes. List the
practices presented on the blackboard or flip chart.
Whenever an item is mentioned more than once, put a check
mark next to it.

2. List of Good Health Practices

The List of Suggestions on Health at the end of this
session's instructions offers six tips for maintaining
good health. If you do not have pamphlets that duplicate
this information, distribute the handout to the group
members and ask them to look it over. If the items on the
handout were not mentioned previously by the group, add
them to your list on the blackboard or flip chart. Ask
the participants to discuss how to incorporate these
practices into their daily lives.

3. Ways to Ensure Good Nutrition

During the discussion about nutrition, women who live
alone and those who live on a limited budget will probably
speak about the difficulty of maintaining a balanced diet
because of the effort, time, and money it takes to prepare

balanced meals. Ask for suggestions about how to eat
better. Discuss seniors' subsidized hot-lunch programs,
if they exist in your community, as well as at-home
low-cost menus and alternative foods that are easier,
cheaper, and more healthful than the ones certain women
may be eating. Very likely some participants who are well
informed about nutrition will describe cooking methods or
volunteer to bring copies of recipes and menus to the next
session.

Stress that each woman is important and that it is well
worth her time to take care of herself. Too often women
who made sure their families had well-balanced meals do
not cook for themselves when alone. Instead they subsist
on a meager, unhealthy menu. Perhaps your group can share
information about low-cost restaurants with special
seniors' rates or hours and discount stores at which to
shop.

If the participants are neighbors, such as in
senior-citizens' housing, they might decide to cooperate
by taking turns cooking together or having potluck dinners
for variety and companionship at meals. As an example,
you might plan a potluck lunch or supper for your last
session, to which every woman brings a simple, low-cost,
nutritious dish along with copies of the recipe for
everyone. If group members are in a long-term care
facility, the discussion might focus on how they could
communicate their food needs and desires to the management
collectively.

4. "I Deserve" Ceremony

If group members have been neglecting themselves, have a
ritual at the end of this segment. Public affirmations
and promises have a certain magic. Ask each woman to say,
"I deserve to take care of myself because I am a
worthwhile person and my body is my home." Also, ask each
woman to make a start on self-care by declaring to the
group one thing she will do to nurture herself. This
might be something like "cut down on saturated fat" or
"walk ten minutes a day starting tomorrow and try to build
up the length of my walks."

5. Mental Health

Psychological well-being cannot really be separated from
physical health because one's physical condition affects

100

one's spirits. Nevertheless, after dealing with physical
health maintenance, allow some time to talk about
fostering healthful attitudes. The Rules Regarding Being
a Person for All Seasons distributed at Session Four
covered aspects of this. So did Isabelle Goldsmith's
article in the December Rose handout from Session Seven.
Ask participants to share their ideas about maintaining
mental health. For example, some suggestions are:

1.   Make an effort to meet new friends by going to as
     many events as you can. Reach out to neighbors
     and other people. Join groups or be active in a
     religious congregation.

2.   Structure your day. Do not stay in bed unless
     your doctor has told you to rest. Get up, do
     things, and keep busy. We need less sleep as we
     age, not more.

3.   If you are able, volunteer to help others less
     fortunate than yourself.

4.   Have a sense of humor.

No doubt your group will have much more to say along these
lines.

In this discussion, point out that many older people
become depressed because they take too many medications
that they buy over the counter, continue to take after a
prescribed period, or get from doctors who do not know
others have also prescribed medicines. Help from doctors
may be needed to withdraw gradually from excess or
inappropriate medications.

6.   Relationships with Health Care Providers

The information in this segment of the session may have to
be adapted to the needs of your group. If you are dealing
with people in a nursing home or long-term care facility,
their options will differ from those who have individual
doctors in the community, use health maintenance
organizations or clinics, or neglect medical care except
in extreme emergencies.

Ask participants to discuss the quality of health care
that they receive and to offer suggestions on how to get
the best possible treatment from professionals. Perhaps

you will want to divide the women in groups of four for this discussion. The discussion may generate complaints about poor care and about being patronized or infantilized as older women. This happens frequently and the women may need a chance to vent their anger and despair about the way they are treated by health-care professionals, who often see them as nuisances. In addition, health-care providers may be very busy and impersonal.

Bring the circle back together to develop strategies for getting good treatment from health-care professionals and providing better information to caregivers. After brainstorming within the group, distribute the handout of strategies for dealing with medical professionals, which should spark further discussion.

7. Role Playing

Ask each woman to choose a partner for role playing. One person should pretend to be a health-care provider and the other a patient. Instruct the woman who is the provider to be perfunctory, patronizing, or not very helpful. The patient should be assertive and insistent about getting the time, care, and information she needs. Allow five minutes for this; then ask the partners to reverse roles and continue role playing for another five minutes.

Come back into a large circle. Ask the women to discuss the feelings they experienced during role playing and ideas for more effective communication with health professionals. (As with all exercises, some women may decline to participate. They can watch those who do role play. Or if you only have a few willing to participate, have them role play before the whole group.)

8. Reminder

Remind the group there will be only two more sessions so that ending the workshop will not come as a shock.

9. Closing Ritual

Close the session with a simple exercise to go along with this session's theme. Go around the room, having each woman wave goodbye vigorously as "exercise," or do some stretching together.

LIST OF SUGGESTIONS ON HEALTH

1. Limit consumption of sugar, sodium, and caffeine.

2. Have a regular exercise routine. This can be as simple as walking or doing arm exercises. Even individuals in wheelchairs can often do arm or upper body movements. When beginning an exercise regimen, start very slowly and build up gradually. In general, no one is too old to exercise unless a doctor has expressly forbidden it. Studies show that people who do not exercise are more tired and depressed than those who do. For example, in a Tufts University study, older people who started to exercise gradually and continued for three months had a seventeen percent increase in well-being. For women, exercise is especially important because it helps prevent and control osteoporosis, a disease that causes brittle and fragile bones.

3. Limit alcohol consumption to two small drinks a day, at most.

4. Stop smoking or limit it as much as possible.

5. Follow the U.S. dietary guidelines. These include:

   A. Eat a variety of foods. Limit junk foods and eat more natural and fewer refined foods. Get plenty of calcium.

   B. Maintain your ideal weight or achieve it by a combination of diet and exercise.

   C. Avoid too much saturated fat and cholesterol. A free pamphlet about cholesterol from the National Institutes of Health, Public Health Service, U.S. Department of Health and Human Services, suggests the following steps to cut down on cholesterol and saturated-fat intake:

. Choose more vegetables, fruits, cereal grains,
and starches.

. Choose fish, poultry, and lean cuts of meat.
Serve moderate portions.

. Trim fat from meats and skin from chicken before
cooking.

. Eat less or avoid organ meats such as liver,
brains, and kidney.

. Eat less commercial baked goods made with lard,
coconut oil, palm oil, or shortening.

. Eat less sausage, bacon, and processed luncheon
meats.

. Use skim or low-fat milk.

. Choose low-fat cheeses.

. Eat less cream, ice cream, and butter.

. Use low-fat yogurt.

. Eat less food fried in animal fats or shortening.

. Eat fewer eggs or egg yolks.

D. Eat foods with adequate fiber: fresh fruit,
vegetables, whole grain products, dried beans,
peas.

6. Take proper care of your feet. Many older women fail
to walk enough for good health because their feet
hurt. Often they have difficulty cutting their
toenails and cannot wear shoes comfortably. Do not
be embarrassed to ask someone to cut your toenails.
Another reason many women have foot troubles is that
they wear uncomfortable but stylish shoes. Wear
comfortable, flat shoes with ample toe room. Enough
calcium in your food intake is also good for your
legs, feet, and bones generally. Dairy products,
sardines with bones, collard greens, and tofu are
good sources of calcium.

OLDER WOMEN'S STRATEGIES FOR DEALING WITH HEALTH-CARE PROFESSIONALS

1. Try to see the same person all the time for primary care so that the person will know you and vice versa. Ask your primary-care provider to refer you to specialists if necessary.

2. If you are dissatisfied with your health-care provider, find someone else if at all possible. It is not wise to see someone who is not helpful, whom you may not like, or who does not like you.

   If you are in a situation where you have no choice, such as in an institution or nursing home, seek assistance from whatever avenue is open to you. Perhaps you can appeal to your medical providers to meet your needs better. Or seek an ombudsperson, someone who is trained as a go-between and problem-solver. Many states now have ombudspersons who visit long-term care facilities in order to check on the welfare of patients and intervene when problems arise. Another tactic is to ask children, other relatives, or friends to intervene in your behalf. Similarly, a priest, rabbi, or minister might talk to the medical person for you.

3. Write down all the questions you have before you see the doctor. During your visits, write down his or her answers to your questions. Sometimes patients get nervous and forget vital information.

4. When visiting the doctor, bring a bag with you containing all the medications you take, including both prescription and nonprescription items. This is so your doctor or nurse practitioner can see exactly what you take. Sometimes doctors prescribe medicines that duplicate or interact badly with other medicines being taken because they do not know what you are taking. So bring everything you take by mouth, by injection, put on your skin, in your eyes, or elsewhere on or in your body.

5. Tell your health-care provider immediately if you are having bad physical or mental reactions to any treatment. Some heart, blood pressure, and other medications can seriously affect physical functioning

and moods. The doctor should be told about such problems. There may be alternative medications he or she can prescribe.

6. Do not ask for more and more medication to sleep. Older persons often require six hours of sleep or less per night. Do not assume something is wrong if you only sleep that much. If you sleep or doze during the day, or don't exercise, that will also affect sleep at night.

7. If you tend to wordiness, bring the doctor a written list of your symptoms and needs.

8. If you have trouble remembering what the doctor says and don't feel you can write it down, bring someone with you.

9. Insist that the doctor take a good history and pay attention to your symptoms. Do not accept his or her saying "It is just your age." Old people are sick because they are sick, not because they are old.

10. During a general checkup or at reasonable intervals, ask your doctor to do a pelvic gynecological examination. All too often doctors neglect this procedure on older women. Very serious, life-threatening illnesses, including uterine or ovarian cancer, can go undetected without a pelvic exam.

11. Do not let any health-care provider blame serious and persistent symptoms merely on your being menopausal or postmenopausal. This happens too often and correctable conditions can be overlooked. You are entitled to a real investigation of your symptoms.

12. If a caregiver treats you like a fool or a child, speak up politely, but firmly, saying, "I have my wits about me. I have a lifetime of experience. It is my body and my health and I deserve full information about my condition, my treatment, and the likely outcome. I have a right to this. I am not a fool or a child."

13. If a health-care provider calls you by your first name and you do not like this, say politely, "I prefer to be called Mrs. ____ or Miss ____ or Ms. ____." Conversely, if the provider is more formal than you prefer, ask to be called by your first name.

14. When medication is prescribed, ask what possible side effects to watch for, how long you should take it, how often, and at what time or times. Ask whether

there are certain things you should avoid doing or eating while taking it. It is also worth asking if a less expensive, generic brand of the medication is acceptable. Sometimes busy health-care professionals forget to give this information and it can be important. Your pharmacist may also be helpful in answering such questions.

15. Do not allow your health-care provider to dismiss your sexual questions or needs. You may have to educate that person that older people are sexual too. Or, if that person cannot answer such questions, you may need to seek help elsewhere.

16. Do not allow your health-care professional to give up on you because you are older. You are valuable and deserve the same consideration as someone younger. You may arouse that person's fear of growing old but that is his or her problem, not yours. You are entitled to the same quality of care as anyone of any age.

17. Try to get the health-care provider to see your strengths. Many people tend to show their worst side to their health professionals and thus end up being overmedicated or even rejected. Show your strength and humor. Of course, don't hide problems.

18. Realize that nobody is perfect, including health professionals. If honest, correctable mistakes are made, give the person another chance. Often doctors have to go through a process of trying different treatments to see what works. Be patient and realistic if this is the case. Medical science has many unanswered questions.

19. Accept that doctors cannot cure some things. You may have experienced tragedy and losses or be experiencing acute or chronic illness that has no easy solution. Sometimes clergy, social workers, friends, and family can be most helpful. Too often people tend to view doctors as perfect parental figures who can work miracles or can help with everything. They are human like the rest of us.

20. Recognize that a health-care professional who seems gruff or impersonal may be very tired, busy, or have other worries. Moreover, sometimes younger people perceive older people as parental figures and transfer to them, inappropriately, negative feelings about their own parents. Older women may be seen as mothers, even if they never were mothers. In

America, some people are ambivalent about or hostile to their mothers and may take this out on older women. Don't take it personally. As a last resort, you might try saying something like, "Look, you are treating me in a way that makes it very hard for me. Perhaps you have personal troubles or are very busy. Perhaps you have not liked some older woman in your life. But I am an individual, not that person. Please do not take it out on me. I have come to you for help."

21. If your English is not good and your caregiver does not speak your native language, try to get someone who can be with you and serve as an interpreter so you will understand your caregiver and vice versa. The interpreter can also explain any special or unusual factors, and this can help the caregiver meet your needs.

22. If you are a member of a minority group and experience discrimination when seeking medical care, contact one of the advocacy groups in the resource list distributed during Session Three.

23. Above all, always be honest with your health care provider. If you present incomplete or false information, that person cannot make the best choices for your care.

24. Be courageous and persistent.

25. Realize that these strategies may not be appropriate or effective for every individual in every situation. This is only a brief and partial list. Confer with other older women to develop additional strategies.

SESSION 11

FRIENDSHIP, ADVOCACY, AND COMMUNITY INVOLVEMENT

BRIEF OUTLINE

OBJECTIVE: To encourage the participants, according to their capabilities, to become active in social, political, or community activities.

MATERIALS: Paper and pens are necessary, as well as a blackboard or its equivalent. If you will not have speakers, obtain brochures from women's and elder advocacy organizations, as well as from other volunteer, political, and community organizations, both local and national. You can have partisan speakers or partisan brochures for this session. The aim is to offer the women a variety of opportunities for involvement in mainstream activities as well as those that concern aging. See the list at the end of this outline for names of groups concerned with aging.

PROCEDURES:
1. Brainstorm about possible ways of community involvement for the participants.
2. Have each woman list her skills and abilities that might be used in volunteer activity. Have the others add to each one's list the skills they might have noticed in her.
3. Discuss how some people in volunteer organizations might reject older women. Do role playing to practice assertiveness in joining groups.
4. Practice making contact with organizations. Have group members write letters introducing themselves and offer suggestions to make the letters better.
5. Suggest that some participants might want to lead or assist with Surviving and Thriving workshops in the future.
6. Reminder that next week is the last

session. Plan activities and rituals
for final session.
7. Closing ritual.

HANDOUTS: Optional: Brochures from local and national
                            groups seeking members or
                            volunteers.
                            Recipes and menus brought in as a
                            result of previous session.

READING: The Gray Panthers Manual, published in 1980,
                 contains a great deal of information about
                 advocacy. The manual has two volumes, one
                 on organizing and the other on programs for
                 action. They can be obtained from the Gray
                 Panthers' national office in Philadelphia.

                 See the chapters on "Advocates and Assertive
                 Women" and "Advice and Conclusion: Victims
                 or Agents of Change" in Life After Youth:
                 Female, Forty, What Next? by Ruth H. Jacobs.

                 The Older We Get: An Action Guide to Social
                 Change, by Marc A. Hoffman, contains
                 sections entitled "Initiating Change in Your
                 Community: Issues for Local Action" and
                 "Broadening Your Scope of Action: Advocacy
                 at the National Level." See the
                 bibliography on page 129 for more
                 information about Hoffman's book.

SUGGESTIONS FOR SPEAKERS AND INFORMATION:

                 Following are the addresses for the national
                 offices of several important advocacy groups
                 that address problems of women and/or older
                 people. You may want to contact them if you
                 have no local chapters.

                    Displaced Homemakers Network, 1010
                    Vermont Avenue, N.W., Suite 817,
                    Washington, D.C. 20005.

                    Gray Panthers, 3700 Chestnut Street,
                    Philadelphia, Pennsylvania 19104.

National Action Forum for Midlife and Older Women, The School of Allied Health Professions, State University of New York, Stony Brook, New York 11794. (They publish the older women's newsletter Hot Flash.)

National Coalition of Older Women's Issues, Suite 82, 305 15th Street, N.W., Washington, D.C. 20005.

National Organization for Women, 425 13th Street, N.W., Washington, D.C. 20005.

Older Women's Caucus: National Women's Political Caucus, 63 Monte Vista, Novato, California 94946.

Older Women's League, 1325 G Street, N.W., Lower Level B, Washington, D.C. 20005.

Women's Equity Action League, 805 15th Street, N.W., Washington, D.C. 20005.

See Jane Porcino's book for additional listings. Also, check with state and municipal departments of elder affairs for names of elder and women's-advocacy organizations in your area.

SESSION 11: FRIENDSHIP, ADVOCACY, AND COMMUNITY INVOLVEMENT

The goal of this session is to help participants to assist themselves and other older women through community involvement and to express their general social concerns as citizens interested in everyone's welfare. The emphasis is on involvement in "mainstream" organizations rather than age-segregated activities, although some participants may be interested in groups such as the Gray Panthers, which are devoted to older persons' needs as well as to broader social concerns. Whether you are located in a rural, urban, or suburban area will, of course, determine the possibilities for community involvement. The energy or frailty of the women will be a factor in their activities. For one person, writing letters, making phone calls to her congressional representative or local politicians, or calling a shut-in may be a big step. Others may be ready for tremendous community involvement. You should use your local librarians and community leaders to help you develop a list of organizations and situations in which your group members might be involved.

Very likely many of your group members will have lost friends or family through moves or death, and they may want to widen their social horizons. Community involvement is a way for older women to make new friends and acquaintances. Probably some women will have made new friends or turned acquaintances into friends right in your group. Encourage participants to go in pairs (or in threesomes or whatever) to meetings of other organizations and events. During this session you might talk about upcoming events in the area and encourage members of the group to go together. Sometimes women who in the past had always gone places with their husbands or companions may need a friend to get courage to go someplace. If your group is to be an ongoing support group or is made up of people who will continue to see one another, you might explore the possibility of some collective political or community action. Explore together ways of getting transportation to events if any participants don't drive.

<u>Speakers</u>

If you will be having outside speakers, invite individuals
who can assure the women that they would be welcome
contributors to various organizations, social movements,
or political activities. Given the nature of this
session, obviously your speakers may be "biased" in that
they will represent a particular cause or political
persuasion. For example, you might have representatives
from the Gray Panthers or the Older Women's League. (If
there are no local chapters, the national offices of these
organizations can direct you to nearby chapters.)
Organizations such as the National Association for the
Advancement of Colored People or the Urban League could be
contacted to provide speakers. Consider the interests and
backgrounds of your participants and seek organizations
that would appeal to them.

Speakers from Foster Grandparents, the Retired Senior
Volunteer Program, Red Cross, and community-service clubs
may be of interest to workshop participants. Many
opportunities exist for involvement in political and civic
affairs. Your city or town hall should have a list of
open public committee meetings. The League of Women
Voters in your municipality or state can also be helpful
in detailing the opportunities for women to get involved
in monitoring and improving government. Such
organizations as nuclear-freeze groups welcome
participation of all citizens. In addition, don't forget
hobby groups and special-interest clubs that may interest
your participants.

A full agenda of speakers plus discussion should
constitute a complete session. However, if you do not
plan to have speakers, try to obtain brochures about
various organizations. The following instructions outline
other ways to stimulate interest in community involvement.

1.   <u>Brainstorming About Community Involvement</u>

Go around the circle and ask the women to list situations
and organizations through which they might be involved in
the community and be an advocate for the needs of older
women. Write these where everybody can see them. Ask for
a volunteer to record and copy the list for the next
session.

2. Identify Skills and Abilities

Go around the circle and ask each woman to list her
skills, abilities, and community interests. In other
words, ask each participant to tell some things she thinks
she is good at doing. You may get some negative responses
such as "I am just a housewife; I can't do anything." Do
not let self-deprecating comments pass. It is common for
older women to belittle themselves because society has
denigrated them and they have internalized that negative
view. One way to help homemakers recognize their
abilities is to ask the group to explore and list all the
considerable skills necessary in managing a home and
family. Or have the women, who will know one another well
by now, tell an insecure individual about all the specific
abilities and fine qualities she has. In other words, do
a "stroking" exercise to reassure the insecure woman or
women that they are capable and have valuable abilities.

Next brainstorm about where all the women's skills,
abilities, and community interests may be expressed. Push
the group for suggestions. These may range from "Write a
letter to the editor," to "Get up a petition," or "Have a
demonstration," "Start an organization," or "Run for
office."

For some group members, only small community contributions
might be possible. Even so, they should be encouraged to
explore volunteer activity. For instance, a nursing-home
resident who is mobile could visit others who cannot leave
their rooms. Or she could volunteer to sit in the foyer
during visiting hours, greet visitors, and direct them.
Everyone likes to be needed and such activities can be
therapeutic. One depressed rest home patient I
encountered had a new lease on life when she was made
librarian at her facility, with the responsibility of
seeing that newspapers and magazines were circulated and
read to residents who had trouble reading.

3. Confront Ageism in Community Organizations

Some group members may say that they would like to
contribute to their community or work for social change
but feel people will not take them seriously or allow them
full participation because of their ages. Acknowledge
that ageism is a reality and this fear is appropriate.
But point out that ageism should not keep women from doing
what they want or contributing to society. Use role

playing to prepare for contacting volunteer
organizations. Divide the participants into pairs who
take turns practicing calling up or meeting an
organization's representative to ask that person what the
organization needs and suggest what the woman could
contribute.

4.   Ways to Make Contact with Community Organizations

Give the participants paper and pens, and say that they
have ten minutes to write a letter to an organization.
Include mention of what they would like to do with that
group or for the community. Then divide the participants
into small groups to hear one another's letters and to
make suggestions for revisions.

If you think it appropriate, ask members to polish and
send these letters, or make a phone call during the next
week in order to make contact with a community or
volunteer group. Say you will ask for reports at the next
session as to what they did. Of course, do not pressure
anyone who doesn't want to do this. But encourage members
to become involved in cross-generational activities as
well as age-specific ones.

5.   Leaders for Future Workshops

Having taken the workshop, certain women in your group may
want to become leaders, obtain manuals, and do the
Surviving and Thriving workshop for others in their
neighborhoods, organizations, or religious congregations.
Taking part in a workshop is good preparation for leading
one. You might offer to serve as backup consultant when
new "graduates" lead workshops. Or you may want to lead
more groups yourself and ask some of the "graduates" to
assist you. This would provide an opportunity for
continued involvement.

6.   Reminder and Plans for Concluding Session

Remind participants that next week is the last session.
Perhaps they would like to plan a potluck meal. Or you
might have a grab-bag exchange of very inexpensive gifts
or messages of courage written on cards. If your group
has been writing poems or journals, you might want to ask
everyone to bring a final poem or brief journal entry to
share at the final session. In addition, you might want
to ask for volunteers to help you plan an ending ritual

for the last session or select one from the suggestions provided in Session Twelve.

7.   Closing Ritual

Conclude this session with something related to the topic of friendship and advocacy. This might involve asking each person to say what she will do to expand her community involvement or service to others. Or you might want to have your usual goodbye ceremony.

EVALUATION AND FAREWELLS

BRIEF OUTLINE

OBJECTIVES: To complete any unfinished business.
To close with good feelings about personal growth, others in the group, and the group process itself.
To evaluate the leader's performance.
To deal with the sense of loss engendered by the ending of the group.

MATERIALS: Index cards. Other materials depend on how you have decided to spend the last session.

If you will be using rituals provided in the manual, obtain (depending on which you choose): a sturdy candlestick and candle; or a basket of flowers with enough flowers for everyone in the group, plus pins; or lengths of colored yarn, about eight feet long for each woman.

PROCEDURES: 1. Cover any unfinished business. See if anyone has special concerns or questions.
2. Go around the circle for comments from each participant about what the workshop has meant for her.
3. Use index cards or evaluation forms for evaluation of the workshop.
4. Perform goodbye ritual(s).
5. Thank the women for their participation. Have a party or some other social function, if you like.

HANDOUTS: Optional: Workshop Evaluation Form
List of suggestions for community involvement developed at previous session

SESSION 12:   EVALUATION AND FAREWELLS

The focus of this session will be on evaluation and closure in various ways.

1.   Unfinished Business

Try, in advance, to be sure that no tasks remain, or that at least only a few must be done at this session. Make sure that you have already done all the "cases" on the anonymous questionnaire forms presented in Session Four. Bring up new spin-off groups if this was discussed last week. Read any poems or journal entries contributed. Ask for reports on any community involvement members have begun since the previous session. Be sure to ask if anyone has any questions or special concerns. Try to have the group respond to these.

2.   "Check Out" Statements

Go around the circle for a "check out" the way you had a "check in" at the first session. Ask each participant to make a very brief statement about what she feels upon completing the workshop and what the group has meant to her. You may want to use a clock or timer to ensure that the statements are concise, or to say that "We have lots of interesting things to do at this session, so say what is most important in one sentence or two, even if you could talk for two hours about this group or yourself."

You may be surprised to discover emotions ranging from joy to sadness to hostility expressed at this last session. Group members may feel happy, have a sense of loss, or be angry that the group has to end. The group may mourn the loss of you; this will be especially true if you have been very directive and supportive in the group rather than a peer.

Be prepared for a certain amount of criticism at the last session. No group can meet everyone's needs or cover all the concerns and problems of older women. Some criticism may stem from disappointment that the group is ending, or have to do with a particular individual's troubles. Conversely, many participants may feel very positive about the group.

118

3. Written Evaluations

Next, pass out either the index cards or copies of the evaluation form provided at the end of this session's instructions. Ask participants to write on them any criticisms or comments they may have about the content of the sessions, the procedures, and your leadership. Tell them they may sign their names or not, as they prefer.

If you use the formal evaluation form provided here, it may be helpful to adapt it to the workshop. On question two, cross out any sessions you did not use. If there has been much absenteeism, add the question "how many sessions did you attend?" to help evaluate any complaints.

On the whole, leaders need feedback. Publicly, participants may not voice any complaints. If you plan to do more workshops or continue as a group leader elsewhere, this information will help you to evaluate your own strengths and weaknesses.

After the evaluation, thank the women for their input and for participating in the workshop.

4. Concluding Rituals

In closing, proceed with your own ritual or one or more of the ceremonies which follow:

Ritual 1: CELEBRATION OF WHAT OLDER WOMEN ARE AND DO

Light a candle that is in a sturdy candlestick. Say that you are going to celebrate continuity with other older women by memorializing their lives. Eleanor Roosevelt, a magnificent woman who came into her own in her old age and widowhood, said "It is better to light a candle than curse the dark." Tell the name of an older woman who influenced you and describe how. Then ask each participant to hold the candle and speak. She might mention a grandmother, teacher, her mother, an aunt, a neighbor, a public figure, an author, and so forth. When everyone who wishes to has spoken, either put the candle on your table (if you will end with a party), or blow it out.

Ritual 2: FLOWER RITUAL

Hold up a basket of flowers. If possible, use daisies. If the flowers are daisies, say that there was a tradition that daisies would tell us he loves us or loves us not or she loves us or loves us not. But now, as older women, we will reclaim daisies by telling of our own strengths. If you don't have daisies, just say "we will tell our strengths." Pass the basket around the circle. Ask each woman to take a flower from the basket and, as she does so, tell about one strength or accomplishment she had before joining the group or that she has developed since she has been in the group. Later, provide pins so that the women can wear the flowers.

Ritual 3: AFFIRMING EACH OTHER

Have each woman hug or shake hands with the women on her left and right. Ask her to tell them what they have meant to her during the workshop and one thing she likes about them.

Ritual 4: WOMEN'S WEB

Give each woman an eight-foot length of colored yarn. Ask the participants to stand in a circle. Then have each woman tie one end of her yarn to that of the woman beside her and the woman across from her, so that ultimately all the women are tied by their strands of yarn into a huge web. Holding the web, have the women sing a song of their choice that celebrates their togetherness. Or perhaps you might want to recite one of the poems written by your group members or one by an author whom they have liked.

Ritual 5: HUGS AND WARM WORDS

Ask the participants to stand. Form two circles, an inner one and an outer one. Have the people in the inner and outer circles face one another. Then have the circles move in opposite directions, each person taking two small sidesteps. That way each woman will be facing a different woman every time the circle stops. Repeatedly, have the circles move so that every woman comes face to face for a few minutes with every other woman in the group. During the time the circle stops, have the women greet one another in some fashion. Perhaps they might hug one another. They could exchange personal messages and goodbyes or say the following: "I have liked sharing with you and it was a privilege to get to know you better."

Ritual 6:   GOODBYE AND AFFIRMATION

Put the women in one circle and have them hold hands. Ask
each woman to say a quick goodbye of her choice to all.
Then have the women say the following, individually or in
unison: "I am a beautiful wise woman who has lived well
and long and I celebrate my life and that of other older
women."

5. Conclusion

In closing, thank the group members for participating in
the workshop and wish them good luck. Urge them to stay
in touch, and make sure that everyone still has the list
of names, addresses, and phone numbers of the group
members. Then, if you wish, have a party, potluck dinner,
or some other sociable get-together.

WORKSHOP EVALUATION FORM

1. Did the workshop meet your expectations? (Circle one.)

   Better than expected   Definitely   Partly

   A little   Not at all   I hated it

2. Which sessions were most useful to you? Put an X beside those that were not helpful and star those that were the best for you.

   ___Session One: Starting to Know Each Other
   ___Session Two: Deepening Knowledge of One
                        Another and Developing Themes
   ___Session Three: Problem Identification
   ___Session Four: Sharing Wisdom
   ___Session Five: Adapting and Developing
                        Activities After Youth
   ___Session Six: A Scene for Catharsis (scene from
                        the play)
   ___Session Seven: Transforming and Sharing Our
                        Lives Through Creative Expression
   ___Session Eight: Sexuality and Family Relations
   ___Session Nine: Financial Management and Living
                        Arrangements
   ___Session Ten: Health Maintenance and Medical
                        Care
   ___Session Eleven: Friendship, Advocacy, and
                        Community Involvement
   ___Session Twelve: Evaluation and Farewells

3. How useful were the handouts? (Circle one.)

   Very useful   Fairly useful   Not useful at all

4. Would you recommend a workshop like this to a friend? (Circle one.)

   Yes   No   Maybe

5. What was done well?

_____

_____

_____

6. What could have been done better?

_____

_____

_____

7. How would you rate the leader? (Circle one.)

   Excellent   Good   Fair   Poor

8. Could the leader improve in some particular way or area?

_____

_____

_____

9. What else would you like to say about the workshop?

_____

_____

_____

_____

_____

_____

_____

_____

APPENDIX

SUGGESTIONS FOR OLDER WOMEN SEEKING PAID EMPLOYMENT

1. First of all, before seeking employment, make sure your health is as good as possible. Never assume that any problem is just old age. "Think treatable," Knight Steele, M.D., a Boston University getriatrician, reminds his medical students. When healthy you can work better and you feel better.

2. If your relatives and friends tell you that you should take it easy when you, yourself, want to work, tell them politely but firmly that what you do with your life is your decision. Get support from your physician, a counselor, or clergy if relatives and friends discourage you.

3. Do you want to try to remain in the job from which you have been or will be retired, perhaps on a part-time basis or as a consultant? Would you like to get a similar job? Or can you think of another kind of employment, perhaps something you have never done before?

4. If you are contemplating a career change or starting totally afresh, can you identify some interests that you have not expressed previously in work situations that might lead to a job? What are your talents, hobbies, skills? What skills and talents could you develop? You know more than you realize. You have a lifetime of experience.

5. Are training programs available in your area that will prepare you for a late-in-life career? Check with educational institutions and associations in your locale.

6. Are you sure that you really want a paid job, or would you rather do volunteer work? If volunteering is your choice, investigate the federal, state, municipal, and voluntary agencies in your area that use and place volunteers. Even if your ultimate goal is a paid job, volunteer work can provide experience, contacts, and a chance to try out your skills. Consider programs such as the Retired Senior Volunteers, Foster Grandparents, and the Service Corps of Retired Executives. Other opportunities include volunteering at schools, tenants' and legal aid organizations, and hospitals.

7. Inform everyone you know that you are looking for a job. Be open to any idea. You never know who will suggest what. Be flexible and try things that may seem unusual. Browse in the Yellow Pages for ideas. But also check with the local office of the United States Employment Service.

8. Read newspaper ads. Check with public and private employment agencies, including those like Mature Temps, which specialize in placing older persons. List yourself with temporary agencies even if you really want a permanent job. Temporary jobs sometimes develop into permanent ones, and at least you will be earning money and making contacts.

9. Remain or become active in clubs and organizations, including senior-citizens' organizations. You may hear of positions through these networks.

10. Accepting a job that is below your level of competence probably is better than sitting home, if you have been seeking employment for quite a while. The money and social contacts may make up for dull and routine tasks. Besides, you won't be under too much pressure at work. For example, would you consider house-sitting or taking care of pets for vacationers? Consider the example of a retired professional person who, at eighty years of age, enjoys handing out towels and locker keys at the YWCA, a job that allows her to be with people of all ages.

11. Try to get service organizations in your community to help you develop jobs for yourself and other older persons. Urge political and community leaders to hire you and other older persons as part-time or full-time staff members. Lobby congressional representatives to require federal programs to employ senior citizens. Remind them that seniors vote.

12. Figure out the peak hours for business when students might not be available. Offer yourself as someone who can fill in at these periods, during the holiday shopping rush, for example. Ask the election commission if you can work on voting days. For example, some older men who couldn't find other jobs have become grocery baggers in the morning at a supermarket. They really enjoy chatting with people as they wheel the groceries out to cars. Some of these men had important jobs before retirement but feel now it is important to be with people and have some structure to their days.

13. Keep an eagle eye on bulletin boards. Don't hesitate to put up ads in public places such as laundromats, churches, temples, and supermarkets offering your services for pay. Perhaps you could cook for busy people, cater for parties, or run errands. One senior drives people back and forth to the airport. She makes a fair amount of money this way.

14. If you have graduated from any school or college, no matter how long ago, you are still entitled to use its employment service. Sometimes the jobs that students reject or are too busy or proud to take may appeal to you. You have enough self-confidence to keep your dignity while starting at the bottom. Retired teachers might enjoy tutoring on a one-to-one basis. Retired secretaries or bookkeepers sometimes like to do a bit of work from their homes or fill in at an office during employee vacations, days off, or sick days.

15. Write a resume clearly stating your experience and skills. Send the resume to agencies and businesses nearby for which you might like to work. Give it to all your relatives and friends. Follow up leads with phone calls. Be persistent.

16. When you look for a job, present yourself well and don't complain. Don't talk too much or clam up. Relax. You know you are capable. Don't oversell yourself. Also make sure you are well groomed when seeking work. Dress in the kind of clothes you would wear to do the work you are seeking.

17. Use the telephone if this will save time, carfare, or gasoline. But present yourself in person when that will be useful. Learn to judge, however, when answering some ads would be a waste of your time and money. Some people or companies just will not hire older persons, but others may give you a chance. With time, you will learn how to judge the possibilities. Remember, also, age discrimination (up to age seventy) is against the law for most jobs.

18. While you are looking for a job, do other things as well. Many schools offer free tuition for people over sixty or sixty-five years of age. Take a course. You'll probably enjoy the class and you might get ideas for a job from the other people there. Above all, do not sit home and brood. Attend events at your church or temple, senior center, and community center.

19. Remain open to learning about job possibilities by happenstance. By being out in the community, you may

see or hear of something, and you'll keep active.

20. Librarians can suggest books and magazines that are helpful for job-seekers. Check your local bookstore as well.

21. What services could you offer the handicapped or persons older and less healthy than yourself? You have skills. Could you shop, drive, cook, clean, garden, entertain, or serve as a secretary? Many people need such services; try advertising in the local newspaper. Are there jobs available with organizations and agencies that serve the aging and handicapped? You could be a homemaker or home health aide. Often such agencies will train you and some even pay during training.

22. If you like children, think of services you could offer busy and employed parents. Advertise them. Remember, half of the mothers of small children work today. Parents sometimes like to vacation without their children and may need a trustworthy sitter to watch their children and check the house in their absence. Day-care centers frequently need help.

23. Organize a support group among elders in your community who also would like to work but are having trouble finding jobs. Discussion sessions may help. Brainstorm. Suggestions or group action might emerge. What community needs are not being met in your area? Perhaps several group members could pool resources to start a small business or service company.

24. If you would like to work in a sheltered workshop for the elderly but there are none in your area or they have long waiting lists for entrance, put pressure on social agencies in your community to start or expand one.

25. Have you handcrafted products or home-cooked food you could sell on consignment in stores? Could you help start a cooperative to sell such items?

26. Get a list of social service agencies in your area. See if any of them have possible jobs or suggestions.

27. Check out places such as nursing homes, hotels, hospitals, and other around-the-clock facilities that have trouble getting people to work odd hours.

28. See if there are institutions for exceptional children or the mentally ill who can use your wisdom and love, if this interests you. Many such places use aides who are given on-the-job training. Often pay is not great but you may find much satisfaction in helping others.

29. If you experience rejection when you first start looking for work, recognize that this is common and that there is nothing wrong with you. Ageism is a fact of life in America. In other works, do not take it personally and give up. Keep trying. Do not withdraw from life if a job is not immediately available.

30. If you keep trying and still find no jobs, you may be in an economically depressed area. Do not assume you are at fault. There is a great deal of unemployment in this country among people of all ages. It is, of course, harder for older people to find jobs because of prejudice against older workers. Express your anger openly about this. Do not turn it inward and become depressed. Write letters to the newspaper, to your legislators, and the governor or join an organization such as the Gray Panthers or the Older Women's League and work for social change. Tish Somers, founder of the displaced homemaker movement and of the Older Women's League, used to say, "Don't agonize; organize."

31. Make your own list of possibilities. Revise it every few months. Share it with others.

32. If you cannot get a job and have enough money to live comfortably, recognize that there are other ways to occupy yourself. Volunteer or keep busy with hobbies. Look for new friends to replace the people who filled your work life. Help others in your community. Swim, walk, or do what you enjoy. Live a little.

BIBLIOGRAPHY

1. Books and Manuals:

Casey, Genevieve M. <u>Library Services for the Aging</u>. Hamden, Connecticut: The Shoe String Press, Inc., 1984. Casey's book provides general information about older persons as well as bibliographies.

Glover, Peggy. <u>Library Services for the Woman in the Middle</u>. Hamden, Connecticut: The Shoe String Press, Inc., 1985. Although intended originally for librarians, this book is very useful because it has excellent data about mid-life and older women and fine lists of available resources on issues important to older women.

Goodman, Jane Goz. <u>Aging Parents: Whose Responsibility</u>? Milwaukee: Family Service America, 1980.

Hoffman, Marc A. <u>The Older We Get: An Action Guide to Social Change</u>. Boston, Massachusetts: Unitarian Universalist Service Committee, 1985. Contains information, exercises, resources, and suggestions for activism. Available from the Unitarian Universalist Service Committee, 78 Beacon Street, Boston, Massachusetts 02108. Telephone 617-742-2120.

Jacobs, Ruth Harriet. <u>Life After Youth: Female, Forty, What Next</u>? Boston: Beacon Press, 1979. This describes the kind of roles available to women in their later years, including that of advocate, and also discusses ageism.

Markson, Elizabeth. <u>Older Women: Issues and Prospects</u>. Lexington, Massachusetts: D.C. Heath, 1983. Markson gathered articles about the situation of older women in America today.

Melamed, Elissa. <u>Mirror, Mirror: The Terror of Not Being Young</u>. New York: Linden Press/Simon & Schuster, 1983.

Midlife and Older Women: A Resource Directory.
Washington, D.C.: National Coalition on Older
Women's Issues, 1986. Lists more than fifty
organizations concerned with aging women. Write
the Coalition at 2401 Virginia Ave., N.W.,
Washington, D.C. 20037.

Porcino, Jane. Growing Older, Getting Better: A
Handbook for Women in the Second Half of Life.
Reading, Massachusetts: Addison Wesley Publishing
Company, 1983.

Silverman, Phyllis R. Widow to Widow. New York:
Springer Publishing Company, 1986.

2. Newsletters:

Hot Flash. The National Action Forum for Mid-Life and
Older Women, the School of Allied Health
Professions, State University of New York, Stony
Brook, New York 11794.

The OWL Observer is available as a benefit of the
membership fee in the Older Women's League, 1325 G
Street, N.W., Washington, D.C. 20005.

3. Bibliographies and Publication Lists:

National Council on the Aging, Inc. The Mature Woman
1979-1982. Washington, D.C.: National Council on
the Aging, Inc., 1984. This is a 122-page
annotated bibliography, available from the
council's national office, 600 Maryland Avenue,
S.W., West Wing 100, Washington, D.C. 20024.

Publication lists are available from:

American Association of Retired Persons, 1909 K
Street, N.W., Washington, D.C. 20049.

Center for Understanding Aging, Inc., Framingham
State College, Framingham, Massachusetts 01701.

Gray Panthers, 3700 Chestnut Street,
Philadelphia, Pennsylvania 19104.

Older Women's League (OWLS), 1325 G Street, N.W.,
Lower Level B, Washington, D.C. 20005.